W9-ARE-567

Profane Mythology

The Savage Mind
of the Cinema

YVETTE BIRÓ

Translated by Imre Goldstein

INDIANA UNIVERSITY PRESS
BLOOMINGTON

First Midland Book Edition 1982

Manufactured in the United States of America

Library of Congress Cataloging in Publication Data
Biró, Yvette
   Profane mythology.
   Bibliography: p.
   Includes index.
      1. Moving-picture plays—History and criticism.
   2. Moving-pictures—Philosophy.   I.   Title.
   PN1995.B478   791.43'01   82-48384
   ISBN 0-253-18010-4   AACR2
   ISBN 0-253-20293-0 (pbk.)
   1   2   3   4   5   86   85   84   83   82

Contents

Preface

Mythologies—no less than antimythologies, which seek to interpret or rather to challenge them—are products of their times. Paradoxically, their enduring validity is a concomitant of an innate talent for modification and change.

The basic idea of the present book was conceived about ten years ago in Eastern Europe, in Hungary, as a direct answer to the challenge of the experiences of the 1960s. The primary aim was polemic: wanting to name what had been considered almost taboo for a very long time. To explore and sanction the mythicizing power of the European film—to oppose the reigning and simplifying theory of realism—was an urgent need, part of a liberating will. My goal was not merely to take issue with the official, debilitating conformism, but also, rather ambitiously, to secure validity and gain acceptance for the morality of the imagination.

I thought it important to dissociate the cinema equally from hollow naturalism and from sterile mannerism. While the former dragged film down irrevocably into the world of vulgar contingencies, the latter had thrust it into the realm of the rarest abstractions. Slipshod formlessness and artsy formalism both proved to be efforts alien to the very medium, particularly in light of the search and experimentation that characterized the 1970s. The original magic of moving pictures promised more elemental, more exuberantly vital possibilities of expression. I was not looking for a golden mean or a way to smooth over the differences between these two polarities, but for the true nature of film's potential. My point of departure was the function of the film as it has proved itself in practice, and not in the wishes and aspirations of theoreticians. Of necessity this function has placed the film into the wider structure of culture in general, rather than into the narrower and elite universe of the arts.

Wherever I turned, I found contradictions. If we grant that cinema can be the most vulgar, escapist medium, is it not also true that its real power lies precisely in its seductive sensuality? And if the film is a magnifying glass that has provided us with dreamlike models, idols, and ideals, how has this function influenced our lives? What can be the essential ingredient in the nature of this medium that, despite the many, confusingly diverse tendencies in contemporary efforts, comes back again and again to seduce us with an elemental magic? How can one explain the rich syndromes of development in the quarter century following the war, from Visconti to Bresson, from Wajda to Godard, from Bergman to Fellini—to stay with European examples only— without discovering a comprehensive interpretive principle, a key that can open each of these doors? The liberating force of film language's poverty, and the compulsive selectivity of its richness seemed to have met in a delicate balance in which the earthly appeared wrapped in divine airs, and, conversely, those almost unearthly powers (Historical Man, the Victor, the Fallen Hero) might pursue their activities only in the most down-to-earth areas. While reviewing the available examples, I was made to realize that the "raw" carried in it no less culture than the cunningly prepared "cooked"; profanity and mythology are inseparably intertwined.

This realization—a proposition?—in the given time/space constellation, may have appeared a lot more daring then than now, and certainly seemed more so there, in Europe, than in America. However, can anyone claim that this principle has been victorious or gained acceptance, that it has been recognized as valid, either in practice or in the halls of theory and criticism? After numerous exciting eruptions, artistic and theoretic, do we not feel again a pragmatic indolence, a slothful resignation, accepting traditional divisions in which tasteless commercialism and academic constipation may meet, at best, in the lifeless mechanism of routine? For this very reason I do not feel it is superfluous to talk about the true duality of the film, even if the present book can do no more than circumscribe or map out this duality.

The innovations in film language of _8½_ or _Wild Strawberries_ or those of Antonioni and Godard had, as is well known, become in the course of a short decade commonplace "linguistic" twists and banal paradigms of the cinema. But, we must ask, can historical developments alter the originality or value of pioneering efforts of a given time? I believe that the interpretation and analysis of the medium also has its own similar and fast-paced history, and what is today, luckily, considered almost commonplace, has not lost its validity, but rather modified its role: manifesto has become premise, a point of departure that invites further illumination.

Rome, 1981

Profane Mythology

· 1 ·

Introduction

THE ONION OR THE LILY

I'm a cameraman. To tell you the truth, in this world in which
and by which I live, being a cameraman is nothing.
I don't really work.
Only this:
I put my little machine on the tripod and do nothing but lend my
eyes to it.
. . . the foremost condition of this job is to remain *insensitive* to
what passes in front of the camera.

The hero of Pirandello's famous novel *Si Gira*, literature's first
film-maker, found little to appreciate or be proud of in his occupation.
He complains of insensitivity and stupidity; of his virtues he mentions,
at best, gluttony and aggressiveness—everything about him speaks of
vulgarity.

"Why is it that in the cinema one cries all the time, or rather bawls
like a servant girl?" Thomas Mann asks. "This is raw material, un-
processed, warm and moving, and it affects us like the onion or the
lily."[1]

THE THEORY OF RELATIVITY ON THE SCREEN

Dziga Vertov, however, writes thus:

We ought to look for our own original rhythm, and we will find
it in the movement of objects. The film is an art of imaginary objects
in space obeying the dictates of science. It is the incarnation of the
dream of its inventor, be he a scientist, engineer, or carpenter. The
film makes possible the realization of what cannot be realized in life.

To draw motion; to sketch motion [and] projects of the immediate
future.

The theory of relativity on the screen.[2]

I

For Vertov, the *ciné-oeil* is the same as *ciné-analyse* because *ciné-oeil* can be thought of as the microscope and the telescope. What one of them cannot see, the film makes possible, by rendering the invisible visible. This is how *ciné-oeil* becomes *cinema-vérité*, expressing a deeper, more general truth.

We know, since Eisenstein, that the juxtaposition of two alien components results in a fertile clash, which then, like the montage, is capable of expressing new concepts. What is the meaning then of the montage of our two opening premises? What sort of meaningful thought can be produced from their contradictory propositions?

The two views seem so far apart that at first glance only their absurd one-sidedness, their impulsive or naïve exaggerations reach us. But the peculiar union of the two extremes deserves another look; perhaps raw sensitivity and abstract orderliness are not mutually exclusive.

About fifty years after the revolution of the sound film, and twenty-five years after the "second revolution" of the various new waves, this question remains relevant. We still cannot claim that we have an absolutely clear picture of the film's intellectual talents or that we see its mental abilities as being concomitants of adulthood. On the one hand, the film to this day is being patronized, accorded a somewhat bemused acceptance that would appreciate everything of its technique but nothing of its intelligence, while on the other hand, the film is surrounded by an unshakable faith that it is the most suitable and universal language of our modern age.

This dichotomy of views cannot be attributed to the relative youth of the film. It is well known that throughout its short history film has fought valiantly for its emancipation, showing remarkable abilities of assimilation and absorption. Traditional arts worked long centuries at their accomplishments, which they then, in the course of a few frenzied decades of near self-destruction, rejected and thoroughly reexamined. This entire progression was appropriated, nay rewritten, by that insouciant and uninhibited parvenu, the film, in one fell swoop; in barely a hundred years it has traversed the entire course of history, voraciously devouring all values available to it.

This exciting age of annexation, however, has come to an end. With no further need for self-justification, film can devote itself to a more relaxed and steady productivity. Proof of film's maturity is that its identity is no longer questioned. Its scope and appropriate intellectual and social function are being firmly established. From this vantage point, we may observe what lay at the heart of film's numerous efforts, and what characteristics may be hidden behind its solidified features.

This study attempts to delineate the intellectual countenance of the film and to seek out its characteristics and limits, its cognitive and cogitative activities. The methodology used is not from the world of classical aesthetics. It has been proved countless times that neither literature's, nor the theater's, nor even the fine arts' refined methods of investigation can *automatically* be applied to the film. More than fifty years ago Béla Balázs warned that condemning the film by subjecting it to classical standards is no wiser than calling the airplane a bad automobile just because it cannot run well on the ground.

If the film has a structure of its own, then obviously its task and social duty must be unique. Today it is needless, therefore, to go on proving at all costs that film is art—the time has come to assert, perhaps with greater pride, that the true originality of film is that it is *not* an art form. It would appear to be only a semantic game to say that it is an art, but the kind that goes counter to all traditional artistic criteria, since its approach to life, to its viewers, and to its own means places it outside hitherto existing conventions.

The film, therefore, is not art—it is more and also less than art.

It is a more popular, everyday, and looser form of expression; hence its sphere of influence is greater. It is more prosaic and at the same time more magical than any other branch of the arts can be. It is the human communication that can most easily absorb "raw and cooked," direct and symbolized, empirical and structuralized experiences. It brings together distant poles. In its mythology it is profane, impiously so, in its profanity, ambitious: it stops at nothing short of mythicizing. Film is a shameless hoarder: it is always in an interfering, recording-for-posterity mood, documenting facts as eagerly as it records soap operas, its activities ranging from sensationalism to the demonstration of scientific truths. Its unusual diffusion and plasticity, however, cannot be written off as fickleness; despite its seeming instability, the film always preserves some solid core. The film has become the radical medium of physical proximity and ceaseless change.

THE SIMULATION OF CONSCIOUSNESS

The above mentioned "more *and* less" definition must be made more exact. In my view, today's film marches in one ambitious direction: it tries to take possession of human consciousness, to rule the total, bustling life of our conscience.

The emphasis here is on the total province of the consciousness, in which the workings of the mind can be found exactly as *the realm of the senses* and *the realm of passions*, all in one indivisible stream.

The simulation of consciousness, according to McLuhan, is a new form of approach, since it decisively breaks with the known abstracting process of the arts and creates a syncretic unity out of the empiric and the cognitive, the conscious and the unconscious. By clinging to the mechanism of the inner world of man, the film is capable of following the diffuse nature of this world. As it takes on the liveliness of physical existence, the abundance of objects and events is no burden to the film. On the contrary: this is precisely the stuff of which it creates its own new reality. The simultaneous existence and interaction of incommensurable qualities longs for new idioms of expression. Film structure's inner mobility can reproduce this uninterrupted experience, regardless of the heterogeneous nature of the component parts. The activating of a new spatial experience and all its contradictory tensions gains expression in film's structure. It is no accident that at the dawn of film's development great innovators such as Eisenstein and Vertov already bravely relied on these embarrassingly vulgar traits of the medium. Let us remember that the "montage of attractions" was meant to line up, in a shocking order, raw and provocatively brutal events to convey the most abstract ideas. But this "eccentric" arrangement has always had a double purpose: it has reminded us not only of the differences between the most remote things and events but also of their organic coexistence and continuity. Likewise, Vertov, with an unerring hand, reached into the trivial episodes of everyday experience, working out his own epistemology by the juxtaposition of disconnected segments of life.

The purely intellectual mode of thinking, in its austere, categorical form, is obviously not peculiar to the film. The question is, rather, what can the film achieve, lacking the ability of extreme abstraction; how can it, with its own means, grasp the workings of the human mind? How, in the mirror of the film, will the *life* of thought appear in its undivided form, which is not deprived of sensuality or emotions, but rather is woven through and through with these strands? In other words, how can the film lead us into the charged field of conflicts and mutual interactions of various layers of consciousness, and how can it do this with the help of an isomorphically dynamic structure?

THE NOT-INNOCENT MEDIUM

If reproduction-isomorphism-simulation is so dominant in cinematic expression, then our question is: where is there room for interpretation? After all, the power of film-thinking depends, as does every kind of thinking, on whether it is capable of examining things beyond what they are; can it transcend reality and conceive of it as a cluster of divergences and possibilities? Indeed, what are the chances that this language, lacking categorical forms, will be able to create generalizations? How can it go beyond direct empiricism by using empirical sequences?

We are aware that the transformation of the camera's truthfulness into cognition has been a long process. But while the first stages of its development were expansive (sound, color, wide screen, etc.), film's maturity is characterized by a need for synthesis. Its earlier means of expression are no longer used to absorb more and newer life phenomena. The stakes are greater: Has the film matured enough to build its own organic structure?

Technique, at least in its intermediary role, has fulfilled its function. We no longer ask whether it is reliable or if it has gone far enough in revealing all the necessary details. We are aware of its omnipresence and its precision.

In the new phase of film the absolute desire for identity between life and its cinematic reflection is replaced by emphasizing the differences and by being different.

The film's age of mimesis had lasted too long.

But how can we talk about any sort of intellectual autonomy of the film without paying particular attention to its immanent evolution? The growing interest in film language and film structure may be traced back to this need for independence, film's rejection of the tyranny of naturalism as well as of the approach and achievements of its sister arts.

In this sense we may indeed talk about a second revolution of the film. The expressive strength of its language is realized no longer in some technical ideas but in the building of its entire structure and in its inner coherence. Films such as *Hiroshima mon amour*, *8½*, Makavejev's *Love Affair* and *WR—Mysteries of the Organism*, the films of Godard and Fassbinder would be unimaginable without this consciousness of language, since the entire content of meaning is concentrated in the multidimensional model of the structure. In this model, the probing of each level of meaning, the unity and disparity between various interpretations, become legible through the several discourses intersecting each other.

Having acquired new powers, the film turns to itself with increasing curiosity, probing its own capacities and limitations. It is looking for that unique, most effective balance in which the economy of symbols and wealth of meaning can coexist in a tense and intriguing harmony. This is the point at which film can afford to break the rules. Personal application and unusual approach are valid only when the language is firmly established and has become the system that offers alternatives. New information, as we well know, is always based on surprises that deny conventions.

Film's second revolution—to use the analogy of the industrial revolution—has brought about, after the discovery of technique, the importance of creative application. In other words, it has produced that liberating step which places human interference and personal presence above everything else. Thus it has created the legitimacy of doubt and the right to question. For modern film is not simply a personal vision but also a self-reflection, in which consciousness examines its relation to the object of its study. Past mere reproduction, it queries the traditional role of the film, and for proof of its existence it turns to the serious business of inquiry and self-analysis. With this step the film satisfies the demand that the Russian semiotician Lotman calls "modeling function," when a work "models the most general aspects of the world's image . . . that is to say, the linguistic system in its entirety belongs to its content; it conveys information."[3]

Jakobson speaks of the "Poetics of Grammar" when discussing one's delight in structure, proportion, and articulation. But to be more accurate we ought also to include cognition in the total design, for structure and articulation not only delight but also enhance and multiply the impact of the message. This is the key that opens the gates of ambiguity, so that above and beyond the direct meaning, an entire realm of indirect and suggestive meanings may be revealed.

This shift of emphasis can be observed in the modern novel, drama, and the fine arts for about half a century now, as the compelling force of self-reflection focuses attention increasingly on itself. In the film, however, this intellectual need is rather recent, since film's intellectual poverty has been considered a given.

The need for self-reflection in the film does not seem to be the result of some artistic fashion. We may notice an interesting reverse effect: thanks to the technique of photography, self-observation has become so irreproachably accurate that it has lent its methods to other arts. The lively objectivity of the moving picture has aroused interest in the direct recording—making possible the representation—of the creative process in the making.

The time has come to call in outstanding debts: whatever the film has lent out it now collects—with interest. If, for example, in the fine arts, in the various experiments of pop-art, land-art, and conceptual-art, the documentative and metaphoric role of photography serves to give us an insight into the nature of creation, it stands to reason that cinema would make use of this effect. A photograph is always an imprint of something that has already happened. But in this capacity it also becomes a metaphor for all kinds of recordings, because it demonstrates how it was possible to make lasting what is ephemeral, to preserve in material form what passes on in time. The difference between the process and the finished work is ill defined; the two overlap. The object of the analysis extends to the very process of recording the object. Just to mention one famous example, let us consider the telecast of the first moon landing. Did not the traditional categories of representation, the opposing methods of objective and subjective recording of events, lose their validity with the procedure used? Who could claim that only the exciting *event* itself captured the viewers? Did not the incomparable experience of *following* the event "intrude" at least to the same degree? What we saw, we saw through the extension of our senses that is the medium of the film. The miracle of landing on the moon was accompanied by a no lesser miracle: our ability to grasp it. The usual methods of recording reality had been transformed into the reality of recording.

We should remember, at this juncture, a basic statement by Walter Benjamin. He likened the camera's power to that of the surgeon, the new element being the disappearance of distance between reality and the operating instrument. The camera penetrates nature, as the knife does the body, Benjamin claimed, and thus brings about a totally different picture. Tactility—a consequence of mobility, paradoxically—demands a greater creative participation, because the experience of fragmentariness also calls attention to the arrangement, constantly making us aware that we are on a "journey of discovery," working in a realistic simultaneity toward the completion of the picture.

What is fortunate in Benjamin's metaphor is that it illuminates the contradictory character of the medium: the unusual sensory power stemming from the aggressive proximity of reality is coupled with an also unusually strong creative-manipulative gesture. The reason for this is that because of this too-close proximity, the picture or message cannot exist by itself. It has to be brought into existence according to a meaningful order. The power of film technique becomes so great that with its help we can glance at a world that is less artificial than any hitherto seen.

"Il n'y a plus apparition," says Baudrillard, "mais comparution de l'objet, interrogatoire acharné de ces fragments épars . . . ni métaphore, ni metonymie, immanence successive sous l'instance policière du regard. . . . Cette microscopie 'objective' suscite un vertige de la réalité, vertige de mort aux confins de la représentation pour la représentation."[4] ("There is no longer appearance but co-appearance of the object [with the image], a fierce interrogation of separate fragments . . . neither metaphor nor metonymy, persistent presence under ruthless investigation. . . . This 'objective' microscopy provokes a vertigo, a mortal vertigo at the point at which representation is for its own sake.")

The compulsory doubling of reality, the inevitability of self-reflection, has a peculiar consequence. Baudrillard asks: "Alors fin de réel et fin de l'art par résorption totale de l'un et de l'autre?" And his answer: "L'art est partout, puisque l'artifice est au coeur de la réalité. Ainsi l'art est mort, puisque non seulement sa transendence critique est morte, mais puisque la réalité elle même, tout entière imprégnée par une esthétique qui tient à la structuralité même, c'est confondue avec sa propre image."[5] ("Thus, is it the end of the real and the end of art, since they are now totally absorbed in each other? . . . Art is everywhere, since artifice is at the heart of reality. Thus art is dead, since not only its critical transcendence is dead but reality itself, entirely impregnated by an aesthetic which holds to the same structurality, is confounded with its own image.")

The polysemic, multidimensional model of film structure suggests this composite method of representation. In other words, it does not follow traditional ways of thinking but explores those aspects of cognition which appear to be uncharted and, due to our changing *Weltanschauung*, long for new forms.

Complementarity, fourth dimension, simultaneity, and relativity, just to mention a few key concepts, may not be far removed from the film's power of expression, since in its structure the film more and more conforms to similar principles.

The borders between artistic and nonartistic depiction become completely blurred: in both cases structure carries substance. In fact, conventional differentiation has been questioned by every new innovative film from Vertov's classic, *Man with the Camera*, to Eisenstein's *Strike*, from Ophuls' *The Sorrow and the Pity* through Rossellini's *Film d'éducations* to Mnouchkine's *1789*. It would make very little sense to try to classify these films. But what shall we call them, documentaries, essays, works of art? The answer is of secondary importance. What is important is that every one of these films meets the requirements stated above: not only do they present facts and truths, convey thoughts, but they also manage, to no less a degree, and with the help of their structure, to judge their chosen subject. Moreover, the model is such that in it judgments are voiced with a full richness of emotional attitudes.

This is to say that these films not only reflect but also deny, build, and reinterpret reality. To *represent* means to question, to reconstruct in a variety of ways.

FILM-DISCOURSE—FILM-THOUGHT

Film is always a story. It is the representation of a significant action, no matter how extraordinary or irregular that action may be. This narrative principle prevails even at the cost of seeming contradictions, since the most abstract idea, thesis, or judgment can be embodied only through the presentation of a "story," i.e., a direct series of actions. The stuff of thought cannot be anything but action.

In defining action we may rely on classical sources valid to this day. No one has defined action better than Aristotle, who referred to its "having a magnitude complete in itself" and saw "thought and character" as "the two natural causes from which actions spring." For him the "imitation of an action" was the base from which, via selection and arrangement, "mythos" was born. Indeed, this is the duality that the Russian formalists, and in their footsteps today's French structuralists, have developed further. Accordingly, and succinctly, we must draw the line between *fabula* and *sujet*, or rather *histoire* and *discours*. If *fabula* or *histoire* is the material independent of literary organization and means simply the chain or succession of events, then *sujet* or *discours* contains those means of storytelling which convey the content. More simply put: if the former designates the *what*, the latter contains the *how*.

What follows from this, and what is important for our purposes, is that an *histoire* is an indispensable part of a nonfiction film, too. The point of departure of every mode of film expression must be the *fabula*, the series of events. The cornerstone of thought is action, because the basis of a story is always the life and activity of people. For the film to develop and follow through a thought, therefore, is possible only through actions. Consequently, the film's *discours* is inseparable from the *histoire*. Contrary to widespread opinion, there is no abstract discourse without a "story."

To put on the screen Marx's *Das Kapital* or psychological phenomena, to analyze crucial social problems, is nothing but building this particular *discours* on a "story." Ideas, arguments and counterarguments, polemic pros and cons must find their expression in the *fabula*.

This is why it would be hitting very close to the mark to state that the process of film-thought will be found in the methods of representation, in the procedures of film-story—of *histoire* and *discours*.

The succession of Deeds carries the Word.

It was a great mistake to claim that modern film had eliminated the story. On the contrary, it has increased the power of the story, expanding it to represent even nondramatic intellectual messages.

"Second revolution"—a realization of old avant-garde dreams?

The distance, either in ideas or in time, is not too great. The realization of possibilities of cinematic language could occur so rapidly because the film's first creators, with great innovative sensitivity, had already touched on its true nature.

The consequence of images will one day become the image of consequences, McLuhan prophesied. We did not have to wait too long for this to come true.

· 2 ·

Means and Potentials
of Film-Thought

It was about fifty years ago that Eisenstein astonished the world by announcing his plan to put Marx's *Das Kapital* on the screen. At the time it would have been hard to imagine a more preposterous idea. What sort of encounter could Eisenstein have envisioned between this monumental work of political economy and the cinema, then still in its infancy? Which resources of this new medium of expression did he mean to make use of?

From today's standpoint, some of these ideas, found in the recently recovered fragments of Eisenstein's diary, do not seem so wild at all. His first masterpieces had provided him with a wealth of experience. In these, as well as in his daring plan for *Das Kapital*, he attempted to follow the dialectics of thought with the tool of the film, "to leap from representation of ordinary life to abstract and generalized imagery," something that would lead to a complete break with the factual and the anecdotal in order "to deal with events not as events but as a conclusion of a series of theses." Eisenstein assumes that film may be a collection of essays, even treatises, capable of raising questions and arriving, via the most trivial subject matters, at metaphysical answers.

A few decades later, similar views were voiced by Astruc, whose following statement has since become famous: "If Descartes lived today, only through the medium of the film would he be able to convey to us his *Discours de la Méthode*, because every film, being a dynamic piece of work moving in time, is basically a theorem. It is the locale of the unfolding of an inexorable logic which traverses its own pivotal points, more precisely, the given poles of dialectics."[1]

Whether or not these daring ideas have convinced many people, the fact remains that, a few occasional and partial realizations aside, the promise of film's intellectual potential is yet to be fulfilled. In this respect, the very concept of thought must be subjected to close scrutiny. According to popular notions, thought finds expression exclusively through verbal concept formation. All other forms of expression are considered inferior and only of an indirect nature.

The true value judgment regarding methods of cognition becomes apparent when artistic or mythological thinking is likened, as it most often is, to the thought processes of the child, or even to pathological thought. The place at the top of a rigid hierarchy is given, unconditionally, to conceptual-theoretical thinking—this is where the mind may best celebrate itself—all other mental activity being merely a transition, a modest step on the way to complete self-actualization of the human spirit.

If all human cognition can be so simply divided into two areas, verbal and nonverbal, then it is clear, in this conception, that the two are by no means of equal stature. The nonverbal is the more "primitive," the less accomplished, for its modes of expression place it into the domain of the sensory, the empirical. Verbal cognition, on the other hand, is more mature, more comprehensive, since it goes beyond concrete experience and is capable of abstraction and generalization.

But none of the disciplines dealing with the laws of logic and thought supports this simplified evolutionary view. On the contrary, they stress the unity of the different modes of cognition, their interdependence and complementary functions. True, the theory of thought, in search of its subject, turns to three sources in order to reveal the workings of the mind: the development of thought processes in childhood (child-thought), the characteristics of "savage" or animistic thought, and pathological phenomena. This, however, does not mean that the ontogenetical model of the mind's development is directly relevant to the entire structure of all mental activities. Although certain traits of the mind in early childhood may seem identical to some savage or animistic thought processes, or even mythical thought, the latter are not necessarily "infantile" for all that, and vice versa: the infant mind is not necessarily "primitive." The similarities point rather to certain universal traits characterizing all modes of thought.

Since thought creates order out of chaos, it introduces autonomous mental structures into the life process, mental constructs that regulate relationships on the basis of a determined consensus. But this consensus, this elaborate syntax, may be of several kinds. It is not a construction available only through abstraction; it may be of such sensuous power as to be able to express intellectual operations in the very quick of existence itself. Perception, as is well known, is not a passive process; it would be unimaginable without active "problem solving" operations. Helmholtz described it as "unconscious inference," and this obviously implies the application of a particular form of logic. Whereas conceptual thought is actualized as a game of many possibilities, sensory thought's strength lies in its concreteness. This sensory intelligence has a remarkable capacity to be all-inclusive. While direct sensuous power dominates its manifestations, its faculty to synthesize is at least as important. Without this capacity we would be unable to decode objects, for the sensory data in themselves are not sufficient to provide an accurate picture. Only the mobilization of continued comparison, relentless interpretation, and practice will combine the patterns of stimuli into a whole—as was first formulated by the followers of Gestalt psychology. And if this is so on the level of perception, it must hold doubly true for sensory *expression*, where all the powers of all the senses are concentrated and brought into the service of communication. This is the reason why in any visual occurrence based on motion, the presence of a recognizable order is indispensable. An image or a magic ritual is said to be alive if it achieves its impact through an instantly recognizable universality. It is most effective when capable of revelation not by telling but by showing.

Thus the artistic, the infantile, and the magical expressions find, almost mysteriously, a common ground: the direct and the abstract, the concrete and the indirect come together in their most disquieting form in these human responses. They transcend rationality and acquire several meanings, become infinitely varied. They are illuminated by intuition and allusion, by something "miraculous" that lives in and surrounds rational sense. For the extension of our senses not only occurs in the direction of understanding but also spreads toward emotions, extracting an experiential identification. This expansion resuscitates the past by stirring former experiences, and we are touched by a peculiar magic: as if transported beyond the immediate present, we simultaneously experience the movement of the past, the present, and the possible future. Spectacular events pass before us, yet they are not merely distillations of past events, but an intensified and enriched evocation of them. Thus it can be said that child-thought or archaic thought, that is, all modes of sensory, emotionally oriented thought, is myth-creating. It is an existential interpretation that produces a most tightly closed order with the help of its own powerful, emotionally charged symbols. These symbols, born of concentrated memories, behave like ancient gods: they change man's fortune, sit in judgment, and do as their fancy strikes them. It hardly matters what means are employed in the exercise of their power. They pick and choose from all the perceptible treasure of the universe; out of the infinite supply of sights, sounds, and movements they select in such a way that unexpected combinations and novel juxtapositions create a new, emotionally inspired order.

EXPERIENCE-THOUGHT

Exploring further the inner relationships of the different modes of cognition, we can point out even more curious parallels. Psychologists claim that there exists a particular stage in the development of the infant mind, past the sensory-motor phase but still this side of conceptual thought, where the power of evocation is extraordinary. This power stems from the vividness of experiences and the wealth of concrete details. Its fabric is not the word but the act, physical action imitating and enacting past events in their oddly fragmented form. The eminent Hungarian psychologist Ferenc Mérei, a follower of Piaget, has called this "experience-thought." In this thought, Mérei claims, the primary carrier of the message is the allusion that is a peculiar transition between imitation and representation. Allusion is a shortcut to giving memories a new life, relying on remnants of common sensations. The true originality of allusion lies in the fact not only that it resuscitates memories, but also that the forces of emotion and will are not separated from it. This results in an exciting play that presupposes complicity on the part of the participants, since identification and experience of the subject happen not only to the initiator of the communication but to its recipient as well.

Allusion reminds us, with creative compactness, of some common experience. This is why it may be content with an incomplete structure. Moreover, evocation turns acts into form and into possible order, which may easily turn into patterns, indeed into rituals. Emotional content gains its charge precisely from this source. Instead of objectivity, an irresistible emotional power dominates the action evoked.

Complementing and partially modifying previous lines of argument, Mérei arrives at the conclusion that the road from action to thought is not so straight as to be expressed exclusively by a process of de-emotionalization. It is not only the obligatory drying-up of emotions or the fact that experience turns sketchy that makes experience-thought readily available for interiorization and for the formation of mental images and then thoughts. There is also an intermediate phase, whose tendency is the opposite of the one just mentioned, one that "does not kill passion; on the contrary, it fosters emotions with which it nourishes the flow of images; it is hardly frugal; on the contrary, it guards against economizing as it evokes meaning with all its details and contingency."[2]

This experience-thought and cinematic expression have a great many similarities. In both, the stuff of presentation is made of sequences of action, islands of happenings, and remnants, discontinuous and fragmentary bits of events. We may not find in them the usual economy of the flow of images, the strict separation of essential and nonessential elements, yet the chain of events shows a peculiar continuity. Only now the selection is determined not by an external, rational consideration, but by a more internal, invisible, and emotional decision. It is precisely this abstracting from direct experience, the emphasis on and arrangement of movements and gestures still pulsing with life, which ensures the continuity of feelings. Without this emotion-laden and fertile soil, the work of the intellect—turning parts into a whole—could not be done.

Both in experience-thought and in the film a certain lack, the poverty of verbal expression, is what leads to experiencelike presentation. But it is also this lack which gives birth to intensity and exaggeration.

While studying the various modes of thought, some psychologists often refer to *raccourci*, the method of abbreviation, obviously borrowing from Jung the concept of abbreviated drama, used to define archetypes. Characteristic of these *raccourci* is the use of great emotional emphasis, passionate and lively relationships to make up for the lack of clear categories and step-by-step operations. Still, we must agree with Mérei when he claims that we are dealing not with a precarious prelude to logical thinking, which is to be developed later on, but with a fully efficient form of consciousness. Experience-thought "is not a 'pre' (not prelogical, preconceptual, precategorical), but a valid, purposeful, situation-and-problem-solving process of consciousness which conforms to the reality of its given period of time."[3]

Let me add that even this temporal restriction is not indispensable, since this type of thinking remains with us in some form throughout our lives and demands a role in creating emotionally colored, personal expressions. This thinking stays alive only because in its images and mode of associations are dormant those "archetypal patterns" which contain basic answers and reactions of human consciousness. Thus, through experience-thought we enter the realm of collective consciousness.

It is most likely owing to psychoanalytical explanations that imagelike, eidetic, or dreamlike abstraction has been considered regressive and acceptable as normal only in the child—in the adult it would be qualified as unusual. It has been treated like daydreaming, or preconscious fantasizing, in which thoughts, emotions, and memories intertwine in one indivisible unit whose component images cannot rationally be unraveled. However, these relationships already adhere to some order, and if in one sense they may seem capricious and inexplicable, in another sense it is exactly this loose, free-flowing stream of images that tells us about the hidden content below the surface. If immersion in one's life history—which is the aim of psychoanalysis, according to

Freud—may be attempted by leaping thoughts and the revival of eidetic images, then perhaps we can conclude that the above modes of cognition may all be beneficial means of a kind of "immersion in one's life history."

Film-thought has resorted to similar methods, bringing together pictorial and apictorial, action-oriented and emotion-filled expressions. Instead of the laws of the mind, which formulate abstract judgments and comprehend conceptual truths, film-thought's own diffuse system produces the rules that regulate the unfolding of thoughts. Although the physical character of the unfolding images prevails, abstraction is not alien from film-thought; it only lies more deeply concealed and assumes forms more difficult to define in words.

CONCRETE LOGIC

"There is certainly something paradoxical about the idea of logic whose terms consist of odds and ends left over from psychological or historical processes and are, like these, devoid of necessity. Logic consists in the establishment of necessary connection and how, we may ask, could such relations be established between terms in no way designed to fulfill this function?"[4]

Although these sentences were not written about the film, they are certainly applicable to it. In the passage quoted, Claude Lévi-Strauss's question is about magical thinking. He probes the potentials of this form of thought, particularly its logic, whose existence he emphatically confirms. He calls it concrete logic, whose necessity may be neither simple nor unequivocal, but which becomes valid as some kind of order, i.e., intellectual ability and urge of classification.

It is no accident either that for a more exact description—in advance of and supplementing the scientific explanation—Lévi-Strauss turns to a metaphor, relying on the image rather than on conceptual analysis to illuminate his observations. He likens the operation of this concrete logic to that of the kaleidoscope, in which various structural orders come into existence between disconnected fragments.

> This logic works rather like a kaleidoscope, an instrument which also contains bits and pieces by means of which structural patterns are realized. The fragments are products of a process of breaking up and destroying, in itself a contingent matter . . . [but] . . . they can no longer be considered entities in their own right in relation to the manufactured object of whose 'discourse' they have become the indefinable debris, but they must be so considered from a different point of view if they are to participate usefully in the formation of a new type of entity . . . that is, in which signs assume the status of things signified. These patterns actualize possibilities. . . .

Thus, these models are ephemeral, in a state of continuous metamorphosis, ". . . since these relations have no content apart from the pattern itself."[5]

This kaleidoscopic liveliness, fragmentation, and crowdedness, the incessant restructuring and regrouping of parts, are very characteristic of the logic of film as well. Because of the union of sight and motion, the film is capable of recording changing configurations and various relationships between objects occurring in time. The more film logic clings to the level of perception, the more it can grasp from the sensory reality of diverse relationships. While formal logic uses reduction—classification always means elimination, comparison, definition, etc.—with film logic the process of classification is less transparent, its ways more intricate. It may be said that it is of a different nature; Lévi-Strauss calls it a "semantic and aesthetic order," which simply means that out of the chaos of things this classification—despite its incapacity for abstraction—creates a sensible and meaningful order.

In the composition of the individual images as well as in the chain of images, the "aesthetic order" itself carries the thought. What we see and experience is always a peculiar configuration of objects, a one-time concrete linkage based on no prior consensus. And yet this arrangement is not altogether arbitrary or undetermined, and it is certainly not free from causality. These isolated details of life mean more than a cursory glance would reveal. Beyond the surface of a seemingly inconsequential inner relationship, we gain insight into a new system of relationships that depends on the place, comparative role, emphasis, or even the duration assigned to the parts in the larger context of the whole. Wittgenstein refers to the configuration of objects as the elementary fact ("the existence of states of affairs"). It seems that this elementary fact is the smallest analyzable unit of cinematic expression. Film structure is nothing but a series of elementary facts. Characteristic of these facts is that they themselves are of several elements, and it is the interrelationship of these elements that constitutes the "semantic order," since, to quote Lévi-Strauss again: ". . . these relations have no content apart from the pattern itself."[6] At the same time these elementary facts are also temporal, they have a history, and their order is never final—it merely informs us of shifting relations and constant modifications.

If structure, according to Wittgenstein, is "the determinate way in which objects are connected," and form is "the possibility of structure," then it is in the film that we may most directly observe the process of one elementary fact taking on a series of concrete forms, always probing and realizing new possibilities in order to exhaust the total spectrum of structure.

Tarkovsky's *Andrei Rublev* provides unforgettable examples of fragmentary, visual logic building a kaleidoscopic formation. Each of the tiny, self-contained elements of the exposition, for example, is a link, but the chain they form is not dependent on a cause and effect relation between the links. The strange belfry, the hovering balloon, its flight and fall, then the rearing and painfully neighing horse, the minstrel and his audience, the barbaric horsemen appearing out of nowhere, riding wildly and disappearing with the same terrifying silence . . . a rational order of episodes can hardly be discerned. Still, the individual parts represent some strict and mysterious order, as if they were not lively segments of reality, but rather the imprints of some vision. These details do not behave like events, but—in conformity with Eisenstein's prophecy—like theses and propositions. Their mere existence, naked and timeless, is more important than their progression. The rapid flow of events, paradoxically, evokes their permanence, impressing us with their endurance and timelessness. But once again, the unexpected does appears not as mere capriciousness but rather as a somber necessity, represented in the order of montage.

A more modest example, Zanussi's *Illumination*, reveals similar methods. The film leads us through the adventures of a modern quester. The young hero is a humble descendant of the great seekers of truth; he is a researcher driven by relentless curiosity, testing matter and probing the exact laws of nature. His life is the quest, a continuous and compulsory exertion that keeps him forever on the move. The structure of the film accurately expresses this restlessness by way of short segments. Zanussi's sense of selecting "pregnant moments" is remarkable. A few compact sequences allow us to see the hero's suddenly passing youth, the small town that he leaves behind, with its winding narrow lanes, the family home indicated only by a gently fluttering curtain with shiny red apples behind it. Then follow the melancholy, silent farewells, the all too familiar country railway station —life always shunted off on a side track of history . . .

It cannot be claimed that Zanussi's images are shocking or particularly innovative. He rather stresses the banality of events. This approach, of course, is closely tied to the topic itself: what we see is the "elementary facts" of a turning point, a boy's maturing. This is achieved by the juxtaposition of a few characteristic fragments. We witness the breaking up of the boy's contacts with his former life, presented to us in a form peculiar to stored-up memories. By themselves these facts of life are nearly insignificant, but their unerring evocation brings to life the atmosphere of leave-taking. It is the intentional depiction of the familiar that alludes to both the commonness and the ephemeral nature of this event. It is the director's sure sense of the cinema that enables this whole process of the boy's liberating break with his former life to be condensed into three or four fleeting moments, and by handling his material so economically, the director manages to overcome banality. With his arrangement of signals he evokes and judges everything at the same time. This happens exactly the way it does in the color-and-shape-changing game of the kaleidoscope: the series of cuts itself carries the aforementioned "semantic and aesthetic order."

THE FAMILY TREE

Why should we consider film-thought as a branch of the tree of mythical thinking? By exploring this kinship further we may break away from the traditional view that holds sensory thinking to be only a timid and weak form of rational thinking. Our attention may also be called to such specific sensory values and visual information as we are flooded with in our age. "What can be shown cannot be said," states Wittgenstein, reminding us that the "shown" world is by no means poorer than the "said" world. Because of the versatility and effectiveness of sensory experience, cognition that precedes pure reason encompasses a far larger realm than does categorical thought. This cognition includes all sorts of impressions and perceptions—emotional, intellectual, dreamt, and imagined "work"—and for this reason the non-verbal modes of cognition are wide open for contact with the world.

This means not only that the strict separation of various modes of cognition—the delimiting of everyday, artistic, and scientific thinking—is impossible, but also that the traditional opposites, such as concrete and abstract, sensory and conceptual, emotional and intellectual, lose validity. Film as concrete logic and sensory language attempts to give expression to these dualities.

A peculiar universality results from this indivisibility of the cognitive modes. On the one hand, sensory thinking is an intellectual weapon at the disposal of all mankind; on the other, it is "magical" and can be used as an all-purpose tool, for it approaches the most diverse areas and phenomena of life with the selfsame logic. Needless to say, this universality holds equally true for the film, permeating its relation to its subject as well as to its audience.

For a closer look at the characteristics of this mode of thinking, H. Werner's *Comparative Psychology of Mental Development* offers a wonderful source. It is the study of parallels between child-thought, so-called primitive thought (i.e., magical tribal or archaic), and pathological thought. The results of the study show a general regularity of repeated and inevitable phenomena common to all these modes of thought.

Werner divides the antinomies of human intellectual development into five categories, which, as he states, not merely designate successive stations characterizing the different genetic levels but represent the basic aspects of mental operations. These are the extreme possibilities, and stretched between them is the human mind striving for comprehension. Werner's division begins with the syncretic-discrete pair, which is further refined and broken down by the opposites diffuse-articulated and determined-undetermined. The last two pairs are rigid-flexible and stable-unstable.

What can we conclude from these characteristics, and what is relevant here to film-thought? Most importantly this: cognition always flutters and balances between part and whole, between differentiation and integration. In the early phases of intellectual development, the perception of an object or the analysis of the external world is a matter of action. This has the disadvantage of not being able, in movement, to separate the 'I' from the 'not-I' (the circumscribed picture of the object from its background). At the same time there is the decided advantage that the existence and movement of things appear as an organic whole. There is the often cited example of animal perception, according to which the spider perceives the fly only when the latter is caught in the web. Fly-plus-web constitutes a meaningful configuration for the spider; without the web, the fly has no independent existence. Very expressively, Werner calls this phenomenon "physiognomic perception," because he believes that we perceive objects in the expressivity of their mobile aspect. Sensitivity to this type of dynamics also implies that isolated meaning will give way to *functional meaning*, for we see things not in isolation, in their self-contained reality, but in their constant interaction with the world.

Could we not talk about similar aptitudes regarding the film? The syncretic flow of images, the uninterruptible presence of the outside world, the introduction of minor actions into the mainstream of events—all these are well-known and enjoyable peculiarities of the cinema. It is true that the film is incapable of revealing cause and effect relations directly, which we are used to in conceptual thinking, but through concrete and visual details and their continuous transformation, we gain insight into invisible structures of processes in motion.

Lionel Rogosin's *On the Bowery* explores the hopelessness of those at the bottom of existence. The camera follows nameless heroes to soup kitchens and Salvation Army shelters, into crowded bars, and through debris-covered lots around ruined buildings. The film neither judges nor moralizes; it presents a series of facts and concrete situations. Individual images in the series are obviously interchangeable, for there is no cause and effect relation between them. The deeper inner connection, revealed step by step, is the untenable human condition. We understand that the most zealous charity is but a symptom of the same and unacceptable lack of freedom that is the cause of the outcasts' misery. By seeing that lovingkindness turns to cruelty the moment the down-and-out "victim" insists on some of his civil rights, we learn a great real about all institutionalized charity. It is fully revealed to us in its "functional meaning," without our being shown every spring of its driving mechanism.

The introductory sequences of Bresson's *Une Femme douce* arouse interest with enigmatic fragments. A pair of hands locked in prayer, feet pacing nervously up and down, an overturned table on the balcony, a woman's shawl floating in the air against an empty sky, then a corpse on the pavement. . . . It would have been difficult to rend asunder and then piece together a terrible tale more mysteriously. But the overall effect is stronger than this tense, dramatic line of development indicates, because the individual sequences not only follow the chronological progress of the action but also suggest the inconceivable mindlessness of death. How is this achieved? By a presentation that, although extremely terse in its language, is shot through and through with an emotional content, exactly as this happens in child-thought or archaic forms of expression: the emotional coloring is inseparable from the message. The more beseeching the clutched hands, the greater the tension between the loud disorder of the overturned table and the depth of supplication. The strong correlation between the contents of the images allows us to read their message. And then the disorder is suddenly intensified, and we take it to be a sinister sign heralding an ominous event.

The sequence of fragments omits entirely the dramatic build-up so familiar to us from the stage and literature. Here we have no essential or nonessential, more important or less important details. Each fragment is equidistant from the core, enjoys the same dramatic value, and it is this combination, not chronology, which determines the progression of events.

No wonder that the first theoreticians of the film were enthralled by the dreamlike quality of cinematic depiction. They noted with delight the effect of objects appearing and disappearing with the greatest of ease, flitting capriciously about the screen, undergoing metamorphoses as mysterious, albeit self-evident, as those found only in dreams or in the most fanciful flights of the imagination. Malleability of time-space, freedom to transgress the natural boundaries of reality, paved the way for condensation. Yet, in the fantastic mobility of the film there is not random disorder; instead, a powerful and effective force finds expression, in which—and this bears repeating—just as in child-

tinuous characteristics. My examples were meant to illustrate how the film constructs a continuity out of minute details, experience-morsels, and isolated slices of life. The two aspects are inseparable: each part acquires meaning only insofar as it is part of a whole; segmentation is a tool of continuity, one of its intermediary stations.

Vygotsky is right in reminding us that this trait not only lends value to action but brings it close to the nature of thought, since one of its primary qualities is the striving for comprehensiveness.

"Every thought tends to connect something with something else," writes Vygotsky, "to establish a relationship between things . . . fulfill a function, solve a problem.

"Units of thought and speech are not identical.

"What is simultaneous in thought is sequential in speech.

"Thought is a cloud out of which the rain of words falls."[8]

Thus the relationship between thought and word, between thinking and speech, is not optimal in every respect. Thought has characteristics that are not served best by words but find more direct and faithful expression through other means. Indeed, if thought contains simultaneously what in speech occurs consecutively, should we not pay more attention to this simultaneity and examine more closely the language best suited to record this dynamic simultaneity?

The "primitiveness" of the film, this necessary limitation, may be a blessing in disguise. Just like child-thought, the film communicates in dramatized actions, and perhaps this is precisely what facilitates the presentation of the *whole* and makes what may not attain comprehensiveness in speech prevail on the screen.

It is worth our while to return once more to Eisenstein's plan for *Das Kapital*. He tried to imagine the generalization of ideas by means of a continuity of action. He mentioned, as one possibility, a detailed presentation of one day in a person's life that would allow the essential features of this person's whole life to surface. However, this series of events would not fill the screen for its own sake or for the sake of creating tension and excitement, but in order that "the theses, generalizations and social postulates of *Das Kapital* may unfold by projecting them onto the plane of associations."

Elsewhere, Eisenstein toys with the notion of depicting the basic conservatism of the German woman-worker. Here, too, we have an abstract idea, and developing it in writing would require many pages of description. Eisenstein, however, does not think in statements, deductions, or judgments, but in images and live scenes. He sketches in picture fragments about the disquieting obsession with "a spoonful of soup," without which a good wife cannot let her husband leave for work. Then, with increasingly freer associations upon the initial image,

Eisenstein conjures up a whole world: kitchen, gas stove, pan, spices . . . then from the petty props we leap to where pepper is grown and from there, Devil's Island, we jump to Dreyfus, to French chauvinism and beyond, to visions of blood, of a cataclysmic inferno, darting back and forth between images of horrible nightmares and the picture of the shabby, depressing home. "To separate very crudely the material of each part and then to bring all of them to the same final conclusion, the conclusion of class consciousness."

With this method—even if in this case the chain of associations is random and improvised—Eisenstein is looking for a mode of depiction that, instead of developing gradually, would reveal the whole of what is to be communicated by means of sensory recognition, of sudden exposure. He wants to produce abstraction out of crude images and simple events. But every picture-event is of a dual nature. On the one hand, it is extremely "primitive," locking meaning into a single action; on the other hand, the suggestive and lucid arrangement of the picture-events conveys meanings to us—almost with brutal force—as a wide, unbroken whole.

OF "PRIMITIVISM" ONCE MORE

But I could quote an authority closer to us in time who has found a rather cunning way to condemn the film—or perhaps to glorify it: Miklós Jancsó. With a fine instinct, he has discovered what exceptionally potent intellectual powers lie in the "primitivism" of the film. He used to complain about the poverty of the film medium, about its simplemindedness—characteristics that in the end forced him to find the most appropriate expression of thought in the technique of the Westerns, in the rapid pace of events, in action-packed twists and turns of suspension and relief.

What did he really mean by the poverty of the film? "It's a very simple thing," he said.

> The film has limits beyond which it cannot go. You can't go beyond the spectacular, beyond what's interesting; in the film intellectualizing is carried on within limits. Even the best film is primitive because its directness makes it aggressive. . . .
>
> What happens in *The Red and the White* [*Csillagosok*], or in my other movies? People are constantly running about, riding horses, shooting, rushing back and forth, and that's it. That is the maximum we can achieve.[9]

Of course, Jancsó is right. Indeed it is impossible to go beyond the spectacular, the interesting, and the constant "rushing back and forth."

But even if we take his own example, *The Red and the White*, we have no doubt that, Jancsó's claim notwithstanding, the film's unusually animated rough-and-tumble action does not put an insurmountable barrier before "intellectualizing." Let us recall the scene of dancing in the forest. It is true that every idea is realized in physical movements, yet this melancholic, nostalgic ballet in the midst of merciless slaughter conveys a more complex intellectual content: a bygone ideal of beauty finds expression in the tense polarity between cruelty and sentimentality.

And what about Bergman's close-ups of the human face that is at once narrowed down and stretched to infinity? Does this provide a spectacle less tense than riding high on horseback? Rushing about and deadly blows are all reflected on this unabashedly enlarged and privileged surface. This is a Western, too, holding its own with the best of them, in which threats, terror, revenge, and mercy alternate unpredictably. Or, if you like, these films are thrillers, since the action is propelled forward by detective work and investigation, by role-swapping between victims and criminals. The heroes talk little. Speech for them is inadequate. Observing these hard, overworked, threatening faces, we see more movement and more terrible storms sweeping across this strange stage than on a battlefield.

From Action to Thought

The foremost means of film-thought is physical action.* This is that unsurpassable medium through which thought may become embodied and gain expression. But can this medium fulfill the role of intermediary—isn't this mode of expression locked irrevocably into the world of physical movement? Is it possible, through this medium, to arrive at some abstract meaning that is not a one-time occurrence?

To answer these questions, we ought to turn to some of the findings of cognitive psychology. Classical authorities, like Piaget, deal with the relations and mutual interaction of thought and action. They have employed empirical and experimental methods to determine how abstract thought derives from action, and the stages that lead from so-called situational intelligence, which is sensory-motor, to the intellect in its fully developed form. But because of their ontogenetical viewpoint, they have paid less attention to the other side of the relationship, i.e., how thought influences action, to what extent thought is capable of guiding action. And disregarding this aspect of the interaction be-

---

*For the intended sense of the phrase "physical action," see Umberto Eco's discussions of kinesics, the semantics of human gestures (*A Theory of Semiotics*, pp. 10, 118–21, 185, 240 ff.).

tween action and thought may lead to the one-sided conclusion that "development" means only an increasing autonomy of thought without also implying that action's effectiveness is dependent on the guidance it gets from thought.

In the development of the child's consciousness we may observe how, through a series of sensory-motor reactions, the combinatory and generalizing abilities are formed. We also see how the *gesture*—this substitute movement which only evokes total bodily movement—breaks off from bodily action itself in order to become the basic instrument of a less bodily mental activity. However, we also witness a reverse process. Physical action in the form of gesture does not lose its significance; rather it undergoes a transformation that also allows it to absorb increasingly more kinds of meaning, to grow richer in abstract content. It becomes the representative of thought. Above and beyond its practical purposefulness it becomes the embodiment of invisible messages, intents, emotions, and judgments.

We may not, therefore, conceive of development from action to thought as something that would free man once and for all from self-expression through bodily behavior and action. Indeed, all the power of creating signs, all its evocative force, lies in the fact that the sign, as a substitute, preserves its sensuous nature. Signs do not lead us into the realm of concepts and images by breaking all contact with the physical, experiential reality; on the contrary, they serve as a liaison, as a bridge. The raw material of sign-creation is lively and sensuous in nature. The more physical this material becomes, the wider the fields of meaning it can cover. Thus, communication based on physical action never loses its validity; conceptual thinking cannot render it superfluous. To study the language of the film is to follow intelligence as it penetrates the world of gestures and physical actions in order to create out of them its own tools.

The analogy of the formation of child-thought, however—and this cannot be overemphasized—is of limited value, and we must be cautious. This much is certain: the road from precategorical to categorical thinking must go through prescribed stages of development, each requiring a maturity of successively higher levels, in order to arrive, in the end, at conceptual thinking, the summit of human cognition. But, what is appropriate to individual development—the formation and use of language, a second system of symbols—is not necessarily valid in another frame of reference. If we focus our attention not on the successive stages of the above development but rather on the effectiveness of the modes of human cognition in general, we find no reason for setting up a hierarchy, for the *raison d'être* of the various modes of cognition is that they each perform a different function and they are not interchangeable. Thus, what is of value in one sphere of cognition may be lacking entirely in another, without either one being defective. The "weakness" of rational thinking is also its greatest strength: the obliteration of qualitative sensitivity and the fading of sensory attributes in favor of structural relationships, formal characteristics, etc. But "experience-thought" must pay a price: its sensory suggestiveness and the generalizing nature of its perceptions are achieved at the expense of conceptual relations and categorical order.

Thus, in studying the nature of film-thought, we may observe a new dialectics between concrete and abstract, general and individual, since neither the patterns of ordinary sensory cognition nor the general laws of traditional art forms are applicable to it. The sensory language of the cinema appears to be more comprehensive than that of either its "baser" or its more "distinguished" predecessors.

The point of departure for child psychology's explanations regarding development is the comprehensive nature of sensory-motor cognition. This is self-evident, inasmuch as the child's contact with the world is direct and realized in physical acts; it does not proceed from element to element but always aims at the whole, grasping its object as an entity. At the source of it all we find imitation. In order to make himself understood, the child must evoke past events and happenings, and this evocation must be all-encompassing. Playing is the basic activity, the "original pattern," through which dialogue between the child and the world is formed. Playing is nothing but repetition and execution of activities observed in the environment. In other words, playing is an expression or communication through imitation, in which we should see not simply an account of what has happened but rather a message shaped by desires and other emotions. However, there is no perfect imitation. The less essential details are bypassed or left in the background, while others are emphasized, brought to the fore. Even the simplest imitation is a selective activity that is unimaginable without contractions, combinations, and evocative substitutions.

But it is precisely in this charged area of tension between reality and imitation that the power of generalization is created. Evocation, however accurate, necessarily remains sketchy. It is fragmentary on purpose; hence it gathers whole groups of phenomena, situations, and events into a kind of prelude to representation, which in turn condenses into an organic form of similar yet divergent impressions.

THE APPLICATION OF SIGNIFIERS

Henri Wallon's analysis follows the process of the child's cognitive development, but it is very significant that he, like Vygotsky, does not consider the appearance of speech a major leap. The genetic roots of thought and speech differ, he tells us; at the center of their development we find not the word but the functional use of signs. This point concerns us a great deal. By following the formation of signifiers, we may receive valuable information about the natural abstracting levels of sensory-motor expression and about the relative carrying capacity of respective sign groups. Wallon classifies signifiers basically into two groups: in one, signals and indicators are still tied to or grow out of reality in some sort of part-whole relationship. In the other, we discern a differentiation between sign and symbol that is a real distinction, for here we are dealing with artificial, culturally learned signs, which, therefore, assume prior consensus. It is not surprising that these same categories turn up, more or less unchanged, in the action language of the film.

Let us take the simplest form of action: an object appears. The child instinctively reaches for it and tries to grasp it. The gesture is the unambiguous sign of a simple desire: the child reaches for the ball or the apple because he wants to touch it, to possess it. The gesture is the direct expression of intent. Cinematic expression is replete with such signs. When a bored person reaches for the telephone and begins to dial, we understand full well what he wants and why. And when, in *Persona*, Alma places the small shards in the path of Elisabet's bare feet, we understand equally well: the signal unequivocally informs us of the nurse's intent and frame of mind.

But let us go further. When, in René Clément's *Forbidden Games*, the children play "cemetery," or Chaplin, in *Modern Times*, tries to tighten the buttons on a lady's dress with a wrench, references are made to past events, which, through the fleeting signals of evocation, we understand in their entirety. The moment evokes but a fragment of the complete event, yet it is enough for us to comprehend it all. Furthermore, because of the concentration of the allusion, we feel the event even more actively. The vividness of the gesture, its intimate relation to the original episode, also implies that the atmosphere and mood are natural companions of the message; they are not something added to the message from the outside, but rather they evoke its emotional content and inner essence.

What are we to say, however, when we encounter on the screen an exact, almost exhaustive representation of an action, and yet the message is different, by far *more* than what is indicated in the physical action? What degree of symbolization are we dealing with here? Obviously, when the young boy in *Four Hundred Blows* stops the stream of traffic with a smug self-confidence in order to cross the street, what is being communicated is not simply that he intends to get to the other side: the gesture indicates his impertinence; it is a sign of his impudence. Similarly, the well-known, banal action of Dino Risi's *Passing* becomes the natural expression of a lifestyle in this film which owes its fame precisely to this power of expressing the well-known and banal action.

In *Knife in the Water*, Polanski shows us the irreconcilable conflict of two generations, two philosophies of life. The contact between the adolescent and the grown man is always a duel; dialogue is transformed into gestures and action conveying the passionate struggle. Daring and cowardice are examined. Which is the real man, the cocky rebel or the wise compromiser, the one pursuing challenges or the adroitly flexible one? Words tell us very little here, but we are accurately oriented through minute episodes that frame the action, spell tension, and lead our attention beyond the direct physical level.

Let us look at the function of the knife itself. In one of the scenes, to make up for his clumsiness and proven inferiority in practical matters, the boy starts an ostentatious game of dexterity: with increasing tempo he sends the blades between his spread fingers while his immobile face shows contempt for the danger involved. The man looks on with a superior smile, but the challenge is not lost on him. He offers his hand to the knife, indicating no less *sang-froid* than the boy. But, with this same gesture, the man also reveals a trust in the boy. The game goes on for a long time. The pace of the knife grows wilder, faster—the knife, the fingers, the faces, then only the narrowing eyes. . . . Then the boy stops. The more he seems to have won, the more he has lost. He has been unable to prove the man a coward; on the contrary: he provided the latter with an opportunity to show real strength and self-discipline. At the same time the boy revealed the futility of his own "values": what's the purpose of bravado if it can't serve even as a test?

The surplus content of this scene of lightning duration is unmistakable: it summarizes the characters and their relationship to each other; it condenses into one gesture their complicated inner world, in which the strands of emotion, will, and thought are meshed in a hopelessly tangled network. Physical action, no matter how naturalistic and reliant on bodily action, includes no less abstraction than the most analytical description, or even a poetic text adorned with symbols.

In order to further demonstrate the scope of abstraction of a single gesture, let us recall Lidia's famous stroll through the outskirts of Milan in Antonioni's *La notte*. Every phase of this wandering is as naturalistic a physical activity as was the action of Polanski's heroes. The woman roams through the actual streets of the city, in heavy traffic and across deserted lots. But the way she touches the cracks of a crumbling wall and follows the play of kite-flying youth makes us see that there are meanings totally different from what is indicated by the physical events. The surface happenings are practically unintelligible; by themselves neither the wall nor the kites interest Lidia. What drives her from place to place, from object to object, from event to event? Curiosity and indifference, boredom and restlessness. Nearly intangible feelings and moods fading into each other, hesitant intentions guide the steps of the woman. The gestures we see only replace, hint at, signify as it were, the background, with its strange, emotional aura. The real background is something larger. The action is but a remote sign of everything that takes place inside, and it derives its strength precisely from the omissions, from what is merely hinted at, from the barely touched upon inner happening, the aspects that cannot be rationally followed.

Here, then, is the deepest paradox of the sign: on the one hand it makes visible what otherwise would remain inaccessible, and on the other hand, we must discover in it something other than what is visible, something that is beyond the senses, that can be understood only in an indirect way.

"The shortest way to abstraction," wrote Carl Dreyer, "is the simplification that transforms thought into symbol."[10]

But where does simple action acquire this symbolic potential? What gives it a wider, more transcendental meaning? For one thing, it is the comprehensive nature of action. Motion always implies something whole, a procedure that fuses intention and realization. I am stabbing with the knife to show my desire to dominate the other person, and I stretch out my hand to signify that I do not want to lose out in the game. . . . Human action is teleological; hence the goal is necessarily included even in the simplest, most practical motion.

The selective, emphatic character of actions is another aspect we should consider. Motion aims at economy; of the many alternatives it retains only the indispensable ones. This, however, puts a greater burden on the ones selected, since they must also assume the meaning of those left out. Gesture, even in its most concrete form, does not stop at every station between intention and realization. It is not an imprint but a sketch, a messenger; instead of the whole, it is an allusion to the whole. In other words, gesture is a sign or a symbol.

ALLUSION

Abstracting processes are generally characterized by the drying up of experiences and the relegating of emotional-temperamental colorings to the background. Concepts are always neutral and strive for ever greater transparency. Here, however, we are dealing with just the opposite. The sketchy evocations, allusions, and reminders emphatically retain the inner emotional intensity and project their tension onto the seemingly capricious flow of events. The shortcuts and omissions of the abstracting process serve not simply to distinguish between the "essential" and the "nonessential" on the basis of some abstract truth, but rather to express, by means of selection, the emotional background and most personal motivation of judgment.

What kind of symbolization is this? Can we call it symbolization at all? If we accept the notion that in the representation of an event—as in the aforementioned examples—there is an undeniable and complex meaning-surplus in which condensation, allusions, or generalization can be discerned, then we must recognize that even on these nearly invisible levels symbols have been created. We have no reason to doubt the effectiveness of this symbolization, even if we are able to demonstrate its relationship only to the various processes of "primitive" or child-thought. On the contrary, it is worth remembering that it is through these modes of thought that symbolism is most enthralling; physical processes signify miraculous, emotive-spiritual experiences.

The most productive and frequently used form of symbolism in the cinema is not the traditional application of symbols but rather the allusion, reminiscent of mythical or experience-thought. In his work on child psychology, already quoted, Ferenc Mérei analyzes in detail the peculiar transitional character of allusion. According to him it is emotionally charged yet capable of generalization; its power of evocation transcends the personal and the one-time occurrence, even in the most concrete physical action. The essential criterion, after all, is the ability to organize. Can grouping or classification be shown to be present in the allusion? Using Piaget's words: does allusion include the introduction of the possible into the province of facts? As soon as the outside factor bursts through the given, strictly objective determination, the wedge thus formed brings about a new structure. For what is thinking, if not the interruption of the outside world's continuity, and then the creation of new segments and new continuities?

Interference in experience-thought remains lively and emotional, but it is still an interference. The series of associations may seem, at times, fragmentary and discontinuous. And indeed the different elements are arranged, in Mérei's apt observation, in strands, rather than in rigid rows. Yet the flow of these individual sequences follows a higher command. It has a "scenario." Cuts and cleverly sharpened episodes follow one another: some are unjustifiably elaborate; others must be content with a flash of a suggestion. But the dramatically oscillating event-fragments, like autonomous blocks or islands, while claiming a life of their own, at the same time remain subordinate links of a chain. Regardless of how well they guard their relative independence, their significance is determined by their place in the total context. The ultimate meaning will always be determined by both the charm of independent existence and the intensified significance resulting from a dependent situation. Actions that allusions create for us are incomparably livelier than the formal categories of thought, and even if they do not possess the dry lucidity and impersonal transparency of concepts, these actions are still, in their own way, building blocks of a comprehensive mode of thinking.

Indeed, an expression made of traces and memories of experience may be rather ambiguous. While with regard to locale, participants, and direct content of its action it is concrete—decidedly objective—this mode of expression is quite open and undefined with regard to the meanings we may associate with it. Why should this be a drawback? The chronologically unfolding action does create a continuity; event-fragments, reality-slices follow each other in a way that makes us recognize them to be interrelated; despite the independence of individual components, an organic whole is born before our eyes.

In the process of film-thought, two articulative principles meet or face each other in a field of tension. Story-line structure, the busy progress of a narrative, is continually intersected by another, iconic, analogical structure of images. However, neither of these structures is a direct imprint or natural copy of reality. It would be much too simple to imagine that film formulates the desired thought to be conveyed by an arbitrary arrangement of untampered bits of life. The process is far more complex: both the narrative structure and the image structure are results of personal selection, reflections of a subjective articulation of viewpoints.

RITUALIZED ACTION

However, even the most individual judgment is not altogether individual; it is rooted in a culture, in conventions appropriated from the social environment. I must agree with Umberto Eco when he says that "even where we assume vivid spontaneity we are dealing with an existing culture, with conventions, systems and codes. . . ." If we presume that the way a kiss may be given, or the distancing that transforms a "see you later" into a sad farewell may be meaningful, then we may discover that the entire "universe of action transcribed by the cinema already exists as a universe of signs."[11]

Eco's remarks are thought-provoking because he does not consider even the most basic elements of film structure to be semantically innocent. Indeed, not even the tiniest fragment of action could be considered neutral, indifferent, or meaningless. Social existence has endowed them with meaning and wide-ranging significance, and it is only with full cognizance of this that we may speak of a new or modified meaning that would allow new interpretations.

Thus, image-events are culturally determined; they transform the "sign-universe" of action to suit the "concrete logic" of the film. What happens, essentially, is that allusion, by means of sketchy presentation and powerful emotional emphasis, ritualizes simple actions. Lidia's stroll in *La notte*, for example, or the passing in *Passing*, can be condensed yet clear in their message only because these actions rely on socially validated collective experiences. They refer to the common experience of big-city loneliness and the aggressive highway behavior that have been assimilated into our everyday life and mean approximately the same thing to all of us. The presentation of these actions would have a double consequence: on the one hand, we are forced to confront the recurring signs of our habits, becoming aware of what our behavior has in common with others', and on the other hand, because of this emphasis on the usual and the common, what we normally experience rather superficially now appears more curious and meaningful. The individual, seemingly insignificant components are not simply parts of some routine action but become necessary elements of an oft-repeated ritual. Ritual always transcends itself: in its most ordinary and sensuous form it celebrates an abstract scheme, the naked structure of its own function.

When a symbolic object addresses us intellectually, we feel that in this object we should also see the representation of an abstract idea. The allusion or ritual offers us rather the comfort and pleasure of recognition. When swept into Fellini's infernal rush-hour bottleneck, we need not strain our intellect to experience a claustrophobic nightmare. But the event's banality cannot make us forget that this sequence of images is mostly symbolic, since it stresses the strongest and most general traits of the event, condensing it into a single spectacle—or vision.

Here we may find the true originality of modern cinema: out of the customs of modern civilization, out of its everyday social and collective events, it has created rituals stripped to their bare essentials, to those necessary ceremonies which govern our lives.

The secret and power of ritual is its generality. Its meaning is so commonly general that we feel that it was born with us, it is part of us. We also know that it is a received part, an inheritance—we cannot arbitrarily give it a different interpretation. Ritual is a social obligation and a shared language, a link. And when we discover in the film the repeatedly occurring characteristics of our behavior, it is the integrating and organizing command of social existence that reaches us. We become aware of a mostly unconscious reality and are drawn to it not by cold objectivity but by a very active and forceful appeal.

This explains the archetypal character of even the most contemporary rites. Archetypes and rites are both abridged dramas; that is, they can be traced back to ancient models or basic plots in which the structure of possible human conflicts has crystallized in its most compact and essential form. In the final analysis, all the symbols of all the various mythologies are variants of a few basic formulae. But their common trait is that with an elliptic technique, with the force of emphasis and repetition, they raise the everyday occurrence to the height of conventionalized ceremony, making it exceptional and exemplary.

In what lies film's originality, its discovery and innovation in the process of ritualization? First of all, in the prosaic nature of its symbolization, in the profane concreteness of abstraction. While stage action, as is well known, is highly stylized in all its elements in which the carrier of the action is not the physical act but the most abstract conceptual system, language, in the film not only the proportions and order of importance are reversed, but the action itself remains, in the strictest sense, naturalistic. Natural existence is realized in direct physical movements and reactions. Instead of stylizing, the film lifts memorable elements out of their usual surroundings, cleanses them, pares them down, and then holds them close to us. Thus we see a hitherto hidden but very expressive face.

THE SYMBOL

Borrowing concepts from the field of stylistics, we must differentiate between the use of symbols and metaphors in the cinema. Because of its "concrete logic," action-oriented mode of thinking, film often prefers the more comprehensive metaphor. This way the meaning of lively actions or episodes acquires an enhanced content without having to resort to the substitution of objectified symbols. The symbol is made of a different fabric in the world of narration, which evokes real-life circumstances. Thus, the symbol is a specific object, a sign filled with *a priori* content brought in from the outside, while the metaphor is born as the story unfolds organically, as it were, from the dynamics of the action.

Does this mean that there is no room for symbols in the cinema? Certain classics of the cinema contradict such an assumption. From film's beginnings to its most recent works, as in poetry and the fine arts, we find experiments that have tried to make use of the tradition of symbols. If symbols have played a rather limited role despite these efforts, it is because of, as discussed earlier, the medium's proximity to the experience of life. Essentially, symbols are made of "material alien" to the cinema. Film can accept them only in the most emotionally intensified, "time out of joint" contexts, and even then, in most cases, acceptance is granted to symbols only as part of a socially approved treasury of gestures or objectified requisites.

I think it will suffice to refer to the last sequence of Jancsó's *Red Psalm:* bleeding white doves, a white shirt pierced through with a dagger, a long lingering shot of a gun tied with a red ribbon. Here every object carries some universal meaning, a content approved and consecrated by our culture. These images, taken from the folk poetry of our collective memory, have become internalized at the level of everyday consciousness no less than the image of bread and wine, for example, or baptism by immersion. Symbols here are elements of a folk community's language. Through a dance Jancsó brings back to life this community, whose fate, in the fairy tale we are presented, is determined by ancient, biblical, and folkloristic ritual; hence, the recurring presence of these rites is an organic and justified part of the story.

The white horse that keeps appearing in Andrzej Wajda's films has a somewhat different import. With the possible exception of *Lotna,* in which the symbol seems too rhetorical and literary, the beautiful and melancholic figure of the horse is always organically integrated into the story. If we do experience something more profound, beyond the physical presence of the horse, it is attributable, once again, to traditions of a collective culture and consciousness; we are aware of an aura of nostalgia as noble beauty is surrounded by the melancholy of the ephemeral.

The more we approach abstraction, however, the more we may observe how the dynamism of physical action is reduced, and how time stops when symbols reach the magical-mythical level. Isolated objects, episodes, and ritual events lifted out of their time-space coordinates create an atmosphere of surplus-experience, in which there may be room, and time, for the source of that light which has allowed us to see the symbols in the first place.

Movement, as we have seen, is not only a major means of orientation in the world; it is also capable of expression, of carrying messages. For this latter purpose a fine differentiation of movements is necessary. In the development of the child we may observe how movement gradually becomes filled with increasingly systematized, abstract meanings until movement turns into gesture, whose symbolic content is unequivocal. Physical behavior, a code of movements peculiar to a personality, with which he translates his communication with the world into his own individual language, is shaped from the sum of the person's gestures.

It is often said that behavior betrays, that it has an essentially twofold nature: it reveals as well as conceals. How does this work? On the one hand, signals are continually sent to the surface; our tiniest movement, conscious or unconscious, is very telling; its rhythm and tension give news not only of a given situation but also of our personality. On the other hand, physical behavior is capable of communicating only a tiny segment of the multitude of our feelings, thoughts, and intentions, leaving in obscurity the totality of the conscious and the unconscious, which is, of necessity, unfathomable.

Gesture is symbol in the most general sense. It transforms feelings, intentions, and the "bodiless" reality of thoughts into images of motion. It lends them sensory form while it remains the mysterious intermediary, providing us only with points of references in order to help us round out missing information, arousing empathy and firing our imagination.

Of course, there are no isolated gestures, only interaction and joint behavior of participants, which include objects and scenes. These, in turn, create the dynamic background against which intersecting human roles stand out so vividly.

In Bergman's *Cries and Whispers*, we suddenly stop in the middle of a rather routine sequence. The seemingly friendly physician, Maria's former lover, suddenly seizes her face and makes her turn to the mirror. Perhaps this not too gentle gesture is the reason—or would this be obvious in any case—that we are so struck by the signs of vanity and greed, of cold and provocative self-adulation, which are hard to conceal. Beneath the surface of beauty now become visible the wrinkles, not so much the freckles but rather the scars of mortality.

The camera stands still and observes, and we are invited to observe along with it. Memories of past events, present tensions, and a verdict passed over both are all concentrated in the man's cruel gesture. In the visible part of the action, we see the essence of their relationship: hate and temptation, desire and nausea.

I maintain that this analysis may justifiably be referred to as a synthesis as well. The arrest and prolongation of the brief moment suffice not only to disentangle the strands of the drama but also to weave them together. The sequence, like a combinatory symbolization in general, becomes a condensed, speeded-up account (we are back to the concept of abridged drama) in which the setting, the explosive clash, and the climax summarize everything by superimposing on one another past, present, and future.

The gesture is an almost crude and literal translation of what mythology refers to as confronting the self-image, the self-ideal. The physician confronts the hitherto unquestioned image of the beautiful woman.

He wants to knock down the image of the conqueror, propped up by a conceited reliance on physical appearance. Disregarding elementary courtesy, he turns the situation into a duel with drastic bluntness. He attacks crudely in order to match the strategy of the woman, which is no less deadly but even more treacherous. The mirror, this ancient symbol, is the eternal enemy of self-delusion.

Surprisingly sparse means are used to convey the intricate content. The rough gesture of the hand, which can be explained only by the man's inner feelings, and the infinitely varied game of the woman's mimicry can evoke countless images. But this micro-chain of events contains, from the first, emotions and moods that are clearly under-stood: ruthlessness permeates every detail of the episode—the silence, the rhythm and tone of each well-chosen word. The provocative red lace of Maria's dress, the sensuality of her lips and her decolletage, the doctor's merciless yet tense and persistent gaze all speak of a relation-ship that would take long verbal narratives to express, but that the film manages, with admirably suggestive force, to combine into a single and convincing whole.

I have presented the most characteristic means of cinematographic analysis: the technique of exposing in minute detail the nature of an event and its inner unfolding. In this way all the overtones, echoes, and unsaid and unshown elements can reach us. We cannot help but feel that in a single act of the story more events are taking place than could be described by any kind of literature. The reason is that we have here a polyphonic orchestra at work: objects and various movements, the minutest details of the external world as well as the conscious and the involuntary metacommunication of the actors, lights and rhythms, mimicry and cultural signals—an inexhaustible arsenal of looks and tones offer themselves to our understanding.

In Shirley Clarke's famous *The Connection*, the only language is that of wide-ranging gestures. The "highs" and "downs" of the drug trip find form in the choreography of broken movements. Feverish activity and listlessness, motor excitement and trancelike paralysis alternate in quick succession. The story is but the acting out of this strange ballet, the ritual of a gang hanging around and playing together. If we are able to distinguish individual faces and characters, it is because the ensemble of gestures also points to a series of individual reactions. Everyone lives through the same situation differently, and the fluctuating curve that registers the collective mood is also capable of revealing whole individual destinies.

Pasolini goes yet a step further in refining the semantics of the gesture. In *The Gospel According to Saint Matthew* and *Oedipus Rex* he hits on ancient treasures that have a completely defined and codified content. His personal vision and interpretation are not achieved by adapting or changing the original stories; on the contrary, he insists on every twist and turn of the familiar tales. But, instead of using a traditional approach, he drastically transforms everything that can be condensed into a suggestive environment, objects, the heroes' physiognomy, and particularly the rhythm of gestures. Pasolini has lent his films a contemporary relevance by using an exceptionally restless, throbbing pace of action, and materials of raw, "barbaric" texture, neither intellectual nor artistic, thus bringing to life ancient myths with a dramatic tension well suited to the aggressive pulse of our present-day nervous system. And the high level of meaning and significance is reached through gesture-language.

Just a while ago I argued that the film has but few tools at its disposal. Let me modify this statement: the scenes quoted indeed accomplish depiction through sparse means. But on closer inspection, we may detect the presence of a number of expressive "channels"; however, they are barely perceptible because of their very close proximity to the multifaceted process of everyday communication.

Visual Thinking

To see: in every culture this has had a mysteriously rich meaning. To see meant to penetrate, to understand. He who could see became a divine or diabolical messenger in the eyes of men. The seer, beyond direct experience, managed to get closer to more distant truths; he could explain the past and foretell the future. Prophesying is but the drawing of hoped-for or feared conclusions based on an inspired interpretation of knowledge gained through signs. This means that seeing, by its nature, is far more than passive reception; it is a creative, intellectual activity.

If the camera is the extension of our eyes, the broadening of our vision, then it is also an extension of our intellect. Through the camera not only seeing but also cognition has become more sensitive and acquired a far wider range.

The camera's abilities, therefore, cannot be relegated to the narrow category of technical miracles. Cinema's earliest pioneers understood well that film-eye = film-truth; in other words, the camera—with its boundless appetite, curiosity, and mobility reaching heaven and earth, far and near, inside and outside of everything—not only gathers data of human activity but, out of the sum of reference points, fragments, and signs, creates a world-image, a coherent view. This view is at once a component of and the result of our collective consciousness; its wisdom urges us to think.

Among the expressive aspects of movement I have discussed those elements which ensure the possibility of abstraction. I shall now take a look at the thought-forming power of optical imagery. This also promises to show a generalizing ability, since movement is included in the realm of spectacle—a world in which objects, events, and people are observed in their visible reality, through their changing countenances and the laws and stations of their ephemeral existence.

THE COMPOUND IMAGE

The latest research has fundamentally altered our notions about the mechanism of seeing. Once it was thought that seeing, like the functions of our other senses, could be explained using the mirror model; in other words: the brain reflects what happens on the retina and perception reflects what happens in the brain.

In reality, however, the model is far more complicated. The isomorphic view does not provide answers to the question as to how information is transcoded from one form of perception to another. Results of the latest research in electrophysics point to receptors that determine shape and depth perception. It has been shown that the so-called stimulus-equivalence phenomenon, i.e., the perception of shapes in different conditions, spatial relations, etc., cannot be explained without assuming an abstracting ability. The mechanical mirror-model theory has proved to be insufficient. Only through the analogy of information transmission can we understand the fact—repeated every instant yet still mysterious—that in the process of seeing, despite varying "input," we receive unvarying and constant "output."

In order to get an accurate picture of spatial arrangements in depth-perception, for example, highly complex operations are necessary, which include comparison of data distributed in time and space, statistical averaging, and other information-gathering functions. In brief, the fusion of different perceptions requires active participation.

For a long time perception was likened to photography, but this theory has failed too. The above-mentioned perception constant refers to our rapid registration of the outside world. However, even in the simplest of cases this registration is more than the simple admission of outside stimuli. The eye always compares. Seeing is the confrontation of perception and knowledge, but not only on the level of personal experience—collective knowledge also figures in the process. Perception is highly mobile and constantly fluctuating; there is always a different background or interpretive basis behind new and fresh impressions. Therefore we may claim that we do not know what we see, but rather the opposite is true: we see what we know.

The psychologist James Gibson differentiates between "visual field" and "visual world." The former is the directly reflected image on the retina, while the latter is the total perception, which, by processing perceptional data from other sources as well, modifies the image. There is no perception without modification by our already existing knowledge. The visual field is produced on our retina out of constantly changing light formations, and out of these we create our own visual world.

Too little thought is given to the fact that we can see thanks to the phenomenon of light. Objects, people, our whole environment are illuminated by light; the changing intensity of a multitude of lights determines the conditions of seeing, of observation. For our purposes here, it is no less important that it was photography and the cinema that had called attention in most recent times to the significance of light. In the wake of these techniques, photography and motion pictures, light has ceased to be only a natural factor; it has also become a malleable, manageable material and tool, and this is how its optical-creative abilities have been discovered.

Besides the intensity of light, perception is influenced by a great number of other factors: needs, former experiences, habits, attitudes, and prejudices. All these play a role in shaping the final image. We cannot look at a flea or a full moon with pure objectivity any more than we can look at our enemy or a person we love. Perception is not simply a snapshot of the external world but a *composite* image that each of us forms based on *all* the available *inside* and *outside* information. This is the reason why no two persons would see the same image in identical conditions. The eye scans the total field of various signals, and in the undifferentiated stream of stimuli each of us, according to his ability, recognizes and/or establishes contact with the signals, thereby reproducing the seen object in his own peculiar way.

And here is where our mind, our intellect, steps in to help, since, as I have mentioned before, perception means not only the admission of information but also its interpretation. As a comparison, let us take the oft-cited examples of dogs and hawks, whose olfactory receptors and vision, respectively, are usually held up for praise. However, since the brains of these animals are incapable of processing all of the information, a large percentage of these valuable data goes to waste. Thus, compared to man, these creatures, despite their refined specialized perceptors, remain "perceptual dwarfs."

The function of the brain is often likened to a quick-alarm radar system: it receives every signal, evaluates and processes all for immediate or later use. Thus a two-way mutual effect is created between the new incoming information and the already stored familiar patterns:

received stimuli are not only interpreted in the light of prior experience, but they also become decisive factors in future evaluations.
Prior knowledge, emotions, and needs, as I have pointed out, do not
exert their selective influence subsequent to, but take active part in,
the process of perception, and thus the end result is the sum total of
motivations coming from these various levels.

Perception is a process of many stages, but because of the interaction
of various motivations there cannot be a one-to-one relationship between the outside world and the received "mirror image" created
inside us. Perception, by its very nature, is always purposeful and
selective.

THE ACTIVE NATURE OF SEEING

But if perception is not a mechanical reflection of information received, then it must include many mental operations, such as necessary
and endless classification, sorting out of heterogeneous elements, emphasis, comparison, abstraction, simplification, combination and recol-
lection, etc.

Rudolf Arnheim, in his work on visual thinking, has convincingly
proved that these mental processes are by no means the privilege solely
of verbal expression; they are necessarily present even on the most
elementary level of observation and seeing.

Perception can process stimuli because it is capable of registering
heterogeneity, separating objects from their environment, and recognizing some identifiable patterns. The point of departure in this recognizing activity is always the selection and categorization of different
qualities. Recognition is classification. I perceive something if I can
identify it with an already familiar configuration, and because of this
I can now perceive those traits which are different and characteristic
of only this particular something.

Perception then contains abstraction. This becomes especially clear
when we consider that differentiation always goes hand in hand with
a complementary mental activity: identification, the recognition of
similarities.

The differentiation of the parts is always accompanied by an overview
of the whole. This concept of shape-recognition is from Gestalt psychology, one of whose basic tenets is that we perceive things in their
entirety and not in their parts. Nothing characterizes perception better
than its ability to correct and/or round out faulty and/or incomplete
information in order that we may see a whole image.

Inherited and acquired experiences have taught us this interpretive
perception. In our consciousness there is a whole gallery of visual

images. Only experience and direct action can help us get oriented there by recognizing—that is to say, selecting, identifying, and continually receiving—new information. But once the proper connection is made, its course familiar, identification requires less and less allusion. A fragment, a tiny detail or signal can evoke the whole—we get to where we are going with the help of surprisingly few road signs.

The success or failure of visual representation is a direct function of its ability to make use of the above possibilities. When do we feel an image to be poignant or significant? Only when it is at once concentrated and comprehensive, when it is frugal with its means but rich in its message. It is wasteful to linger over familiar and obvious connections; it is enough for us to see (or hear) clattering train wheels to know that we are dealing with a journey; it will suffice to see a closing cell door, a pointed gun, patrolling police, hands clasped in prayer . . . we could go on endlessly. In our memory all the relevant knowledge and stored-up images immediately begin to function. With the help of our experiences we fill in the missing parts in a fraction of a second. As I have said earlier, the past facilitates the perception of the present; without activating old stimuli we could not recognize and process new ones. But what exactly happens when, as if by magic, memories come to life? With lightning speed we perform several tasks, such as superimposing, identifying, repelling, and modifying. It is interesting that we mobilize not only visual memories; other experiences—kinesthetic, tactile, and auditory—also play a role. But there is no doubt that memory preserves information and impressions, first of all, in images, in eidetic forms.

Human perception is, to a certain extent, synesthetic. Chances are that hearing a rattling wagon will induce the seeing of the wagon, and vice versa. On this basis the early pioneers of the silent film created the "silent sound phenomenon." Eisenstein, for example, substituted a super close-up of a siren for its shrill whistle, or demonstrated the rumbling of a crowd by its irresistible, driving march. What in those days was born of necessity has now become a gift, in the form of clever omissions and laconic modes of expression. Out of the wide selection available to it, the film can juggle, exchange, and replace parts, and compose in most unusual ways. The sparser the means film uses, the more active its audience's participation will be.

One may get the impression that this collaboration between cinema and its audience works only when dealing with culturally and historically approved signs whose meanings have been fixed, and that confusion will set in the moment we encounter less known or hitherto unseen relationships. This is true only to a degree, for cinema can present nothing whose components do not already exist, fully formed, somewhere in the world. It is true that the supply of film's visual means is endless, and therefore new image combinations are constantly being created, with each new combination able to assume a new meaning. Yet, our understanding of the new images is always assured. How is this achieved? Rather simply. During the course of events a given phenomenon is discovered that, at first glance, may be nothing more than a hazy core, the thing interpreting itself. But once this has happened, the slightest, most fragmentary allusion or repetition may serve as a basis for further interpretation. Relying on the sign-significance relationship, the narration further builds and modifies the desired thought.

In Edouard Luntz's *Immature Hearts* there is a vacant lot at whose edges steel beams are reaching toward the sky. A gang of boys spend their time hanging around these beams. From here—crawling, sitting, straddling the beams—they take their turns raping girls, one of the ceremonies of their communal life together. We see the strange structure once at the beginning of the film, but when the same scene reappears, with the same boys swinging with feline dexterity on the same beams, who would not understand the ritual involved? No matter how sketchy the reminder, the appearance of the images alone already foreshadows a whole chain of events. In other words, anticipation puts us in a state of intellectual alert: we know exactly what will happen although we have seen nothing of it.

VISUAL CONCEPTS

Those memory images which gain strength by repetition we call *visual concepts,* for at the bottom of their being etched into our memory lie the mental operations of abstraction and generalization. We record a configuration striving for what is essential, a pattern that contains the most important characteristics of a given phenomenon— only we do this not by naming and classifying but through the sensory-active occurrence itself. An increasingly permanent meaning is attached to one-time arrangements, and the condensation of images as well as the crystallization of characteristics into models lead to abstraction and more generalizing thought. In visual-action-bound representation, repetition is the starting point of mental activity, the basis of logical arrangement.

Here is the first station of abstraction. Things, including the simplest objects, are always seen in their context of past and possible future history. This is how we perceive changes and permanence. Only against the background of permanence is it possible to understand the different aspects of things as deviations, modifications, and even distortions of a unique configuration.

In seeing, we find the eternal opposition of change and permanence. Changes appear as the accidental detours of similarities, and conversely: in terms of perception permanence means the process of ceaseless change.

Past experience and memory have importance insofar as they provide a basis for comparison, for registering changes. This means that the realization of deviation not only allows the discovery of, but forcefully calls forth, the original structure. The basic structure determines identification or interpretation; it complements and rounds out perception. Looking at it from the opposite point of view: through variations we gain a deeper insight and understanding of the basic structure, the fundamental thought.

Buñuel's *The Exterminating Angel* opens with an eerie scene for which there is no rational explanation. Suddenly a curse settles on one of the mansions on Providence Road, and the guests inside cannot cross the threshold in order to leave. We see no diabolical tricks, magic, or any secret signs; all that happens is that people become confused as if a wall stood in their way. They are condemned to captivity in the accursed house. Then, at the end of the film, the scene is repeated. And again, we notice no tricks, magic, or secret signs. All that happens is that people become confused as if a wall stood in their way, and they cannot step over the threshold. It is true that we are no longer in the mansion itself but in its chapel; the guests are not the ones we had seen earlier, and instead of facing us, they now have their backs in our direction as they push and shove, trying to leave this bewitched house of God. But, despite the changed setting and circumstances, every essential feature is the same. These people are cursed and we understand their fate.

To see, that is to speak in images, in a visual language, means collating and comparing the essential structures of things. Not only thought works with structures, but so does perception. Not only thought refers things to the context of time-space relationships, but so does perception. Indeed, "the soul never thinks without images," but this is possible only because the images themselves are highly abstracted. In our consciousness visual forms live and are stored as visual concepts.

If we agree that thought affects seeing and vice versa, then we may ask, along with Arnheim, is it possible that these two are qualitatively different from one another? Seeing is the most articulate and richest mode of sensory perception: we receive more than eighty percent of all our information through our eyes. This is why seeing is naturally the foremost medium of thought. The activation of our senses is indispensable to mental operations, but we must not neglect the other side of the relationship: the mind guides and permeates sensory perception; the elements of thought in perception, and perception's elements in thought are complementary parts. They unify human perception, but their common denominator is the presence of abstraction in all modes of perception.

We must now define abstraction more accurately. The dichotomy that sees pivots of tangible and intangible, or physical and mental realities in the concrete-abstract opposition is false. Any object may be abstract as long as it is capable of representing a content beyond itself or expressing something by way of substitution.

Is the church bell in *Rubljov*'s famous bell-founding scene an object of reality? Although it is handled in the most tangible manner—its heavy body is revealed in long and detailed shots; its material and every screw is shown us in plastic and enlarged forms—it is still questionable whether we are really dealing with the founding of a bell. Is this bell, despite its overwhelming concreteness, not a most abstract symbol as well?

This bell then is a substitute for something; laden with abstraction, it is an intangible, spiritual symbol, but what makes this function possible is the bell's physical presence, its materiality.

Abstraction is fertile when it is generative. The first step is always concept formation; then comes generalization. Concepts themselves, however, may be of two kinds: collective or type-concepts, depending on whether they are of an all-inclusive nature or they emphasize the structural essence of one aspect of the whole. Visual concepts are closer to the latter, since in them not the synthesizing but rather the suggestive, evocative power dominates.

Let me further illustrate my reasoning. It is obvious that the film cannot represent, for example, a table, a dog, or a horse as a collective concept. But if the film uses the above described method—emphasizing the identical structural similarities of different objects or phenomena—the many similarities through individual variations will also lead to a comprehensive whole. Would it not be correct to say that the accumulation of so many actual, concrete appearances, situations, and functions in Zoltán Husarik's *Elegy* does give us the abstract concept of the horse—or rather the fate of the horse—by breaking down and bringing to life abstractions?

The peculiarity of visual concepts is that they are capable of abstraction only in concrete forms.

DETAILS ENLARGED

The most frequently used method of sensory abstraction, of creating concrete concepts, is the emphasis and enlargement of details. The basis of every poetic metaphor is a *pars pro toto*, the principle of synecdoche, which means a change of place, a substitution.

I have already mentioned that the film brings to us the whole while letting the parts live their own lives. Cinema's heterogeneity is nothing but an exceptionally intensified perception of the whole, as it is described by Gestalt psychology. That is to say that, although our encounter is always first of all with a totality, we then proceed to break it down and restructure it.

Lifting out and emphasizing details is, of course, very suggestive. What is the basis of this great evocative power? First, it is the tyrannical directing of our attention and the deliberate omissions that may become effective as a mobilizing suggestion. It is the part that is responsible for and summons to our imagination the whole.

Wajda's *Wedding* relies throughout almost exclusively on this method. It is full of miniature fragments, shards of the sweeping euphoria of the dance. Even faces and gestures are broken down into smaller elements: an exploding patch of color, the sweat glittering on everybody's face, the darkness of the ominous night. . . .

The sharp emphasis results in increasingly better described visual concepts. The fancy folk-dresses and ornaments, headdresses, and countless layers of weighty lace all act as poetic elements of universal meaning applied retroactively. Their function is far more than simple narrative representation. They become the carefully constructed and well-prepared road signs of a passionately communicative line of thought. Out of the tense and unusual coupling of visual concepts are born many metaphors—notice the unexpected connection between a perspiring face and the emblem of the folklore museum, the strange riders and the enchanted, haunting landscape. . . .

In Károly Makk's *Catsplay*, memory's excursions out of the present are indicated by persistently returning objects and details of interiors: savory food on a plate, a fluttering ribbon of a hat, old and yellowed photographs, the slender arch of a bridge railing—the time-space reality of a bygone life are established by these radiating details.

DEVELOPMENT OF SPACE PERCEPTION

The emphasis of details, although a poet's tool throughout the ages, is linked to new concepts of space. Today a separate science deals with the historical, sociological, and psychological changes of space perception. Proxemics classifies experiences in terms of distances between man and objects. Its most important discovery is that our sense and awareness of space do not depend on physiological factors alone, but also on our culture. Hence, space perception varies in different eras and cultural spheres.

In his witty booklet, *The Hidden Dimension*, Edward Hall lists numerous examples to illustrate the differences between occidental and oriental space perception. The former, Hall says, senses the objects and not the space between them, while in Japan, for example, space is so honored that there is a special name for the interval between objects. (This observation may help us better to understand the kinetic language of certain Japanese films. The oft-mentioned "ballet," which so clearly distinguishes the oriental heroes' movements from those of their European counterparts, may possibly be explained by the oriental spatial experience: this is the reason why there are no empty or neutral gestures, only significant ones, where every inch of progression is highly articulated and carefully shaped.)

More important, however, is that during the course of historical development—as witness the fine arts—perception itself has undergone changes. Men of antiquity experienced space differently from us; Egyptian, Greek, and then Roman architecture clearly shows that man learned rather gradually to see himself in space. The Renaissance, however, gives evidence most emphatically of man's becoming aware of his space perception: the greatest discovery of that age, perspective, strove to represent three-dimensional space. It is a different matter that with the system of linear, single-viewpoint perspective the Renaissance also acquired the burden of this system's inner contradictions—this static view of space brought about the purest two-dimensional model of space. It is no accident that its greatest practitioners had continually modified and loosened the rigid mathematical rules of perspective, which, for example, made the height of man a strict function of distance. The baroque period had also attempted to express a more dynamic spatial experience, but it took centuries until the compositional principle based on the vanishing point was replaced by a more flexible view of space perception.

On the stage, it took a whole revolution early in this century to free the world stuck behind borders, wings, and perspective-flats. First came the impressionists, attacking with light, discovering the aura surrounding objects, and giving us the perspective of air and air-space. Then came the surrealists and abstractionists, scandalizing and provoking audiences with daring demonstrations of new space perceptions. Chagall created an unusual sense of depth by a renewed use of pure colors (especially red, blue, and green); Braque endeavored to represent a tactile space by his peculiar treatment of surfaces; Klee took pains to relate time to space and tried to grasp the dynamics of changing space due to motion. The various worlds of perception, however, differ, first of all, in their structural composition—what is being modified is the combination, proportion, and hierarchy of the sensory impressions.

Pierre Francastel points out the exact historical moment when modern spatial experience had won acceptance. The sum total of changing experiences of space always carries both individual and social significance, he maintains; it is at once a structure and a temporary collection of symbolic forms. New space perception begins with the exploding of the scenographic system of space, allowing the value of the fragment to be realized: the concept of plastic composition is transferred from the whole to the part, while our sensitivity to details directs attention toward fragments and structures.

The time of vertical planes, separations similar to the multitiered theater, are over, Francastel claims. By changing its own position, the eye changes the structure of what it sees. The rule that one can only strive for the presentation of the whole no longer holds; the autonomous detail is discovered by relying on a new perception of our contemporary world.

Up to now space has been thought of as a neutral, dead background, an indifferent frame providing room for various objects, or, as Francastel so graphically put it, "for object-structures to submerge in it." In modern times man has more and more arrogantly stepped into the space of reality. The theatrical, distant point of observation has given way to a variously approachable and changeable, dynamic space conception. This, of course, did not take place independently from modern science's interpretation, which also calls space active, since it determines the behavior of objects moving about in it. It is neither passive nor empty—not a cube of air so ideally composed by classical geometry; space is an agent urging all bodies in it to progress; it is a field that leads.

This space is neither perceptional nor experiential. It cannot be reached directly with our senses alone, but, thanks to the mobile camera, it has become gradually conquerable. Whatever our imagination and knowledge had managed to process was, with the help of the sciences whose task it was to penetrate matter, sooner or later also revealed by technology and human intellect. It was a long road from the mechanical concept of space—which, at best, sought relationships between objects, and reached a single-viewpoint perspective—to the concept of pluralistic and simultaneous space perception. These changes in space experience, and they cannot be overemphasized, are not, primarily, of artistic or aesthetic significance. No less important is their link with science and technology and with our modern way of thinking and looking at reality in general. There is a role here for the cinema too, which, in its technique and peculiar expressive ability, is trying to cope with the needs of our age. Looking over this most sketchy discussion of historical development, I feel that an inevitable necessity produced the demand for a medium that would contain time and space, fragments and continuity, details and dynamic flow of events, and mold them into a unified whole.

Of course, the cinema itself has had to undergo a certain historical development in order to work out the ways of handling the new modes of time-space relationships. The starting point was the recording and reproduction of movement. Based on this achievement, the camera, not unlike man wanting to know his world, has had to learn the tricks of orientation and of positioning itself in space, and, later on, the increasingly more complicated ways of self-expression. In the gradual acquisition of space-channeling ability we encounter surprising parallels between the cinema and child-thinking. This is no accident. Where else, looking for the tradition of image-creating, would we find kindred signs, if not in the "magical" past of ontogenetical and phylogenetical development?

Thanks to Piaget and others, today we are thoroughly familiar with the stages of space perception as it develops in the child. Instinctive space-time sensations, then images, various space and time structures, are at the service of sensory-motor expression. We are told that space— at first not the locale of possible courses of occurrence—is inseparable from realized situations. The difficulty lies in the fact that the virtual, the possible occurrence is not easily separated from reality. Spatial concreteness, being fixed in space, proves superior to thinking in possibilities; the image is stronger than the concepts. When space slowly detaches itself from objects, or, more accurately, objects detach themselves from space, they may become free-moving and manageable images on the one hand, and, on the other, space may turn into a field in which the imagination can roam free, and objects, separate from it, may move about in it without losing their own identity.

In the nascent, unanalytical stages of perception, space may appear to be absolute, as if absorbed by the objects in it. It is hard to separate objects from their environment. Later the child learns to structure the undivided whole. The formulae of situational arrangements, however, are influenced not only by space but also by time. Space exists in a state of dynamic relationships, whose changes unfold in time. When space is gradually freed from its stationary restrictions, so that the observer is able to experience in it the mixture of the ephemeral and the permanent, then time asserts itself and facilitates the arrangement of the different groupings.

In real action as well as in the arts imitating action, it is time that organizes, articulates, condenses, and enlarges space.

The space conception of primitive man, according to Werner, is very similar to what was described above. It is also an undivided perception, elementary and concrete, ruled by emotional factors—which is the reason why it cannot be measured. It is egocentric and anthropomorphic. Primitive man, like the child, is unable to separate object from space. For him the two are so organically intertwined that only in a direct-contact situation of great emotional significance is he able to form a somewhat vague image of space.

The space conception of mythical thinking, however, is more complex. It is highly organized, since it is in a spatial context that mythical thinking attempts to visualize sacred experience and rituals that dictate the rules of social existence. Yet even this fascinatingly choreographed perception, which so sensitively uses and interprets space, does not lean toward a geometric order, but remains dynamic and direct.

Edward Hall nicely illustrates the ineluctable and emotional versatility of space perception. It is well known that nature and its phenomena are more finely perceived and experienced by "primitive" than by "civilized" peoples. This is reflected in the rich vocabulary of the former regarding nature, while we can hardly find words with which they describe abstract concepts, including space. Thus, it is not so much objects but rather various relationships and sensory signs with which they orientate themselves in space. They express their world by naming odors and sounds, by describing with infinite nuances the varieties of wind or snow, for example.

This is rather illuminating in analyzing cinematic space, for it reminds us that there is no pure visuality. Orientation in space may well be the result of a number of other sensory stimuli, on which the film can rely with certainty. And further, there is once again a balance reached between gains and losses: whatever cinema's sensory language lacks—stylized and abstract structure of space, for instance—it makes up for with a generous supply of heterogeneous sensory qualities. The acoustic, kinesthetic, and arrhythmic experiences may produce, with their own means, the illusion of depth or even the monumentality of space.

I have already mentioned that the film needed certain developmental experiences in order to produce its own unique method of dealing with space. One process in this development, called the "emancipation of the camera," strikingly resembles the child's growing awareness of space. Here, too, empiricism characterizes the beginning stages. Movement is nothing but the necessary change of position in order to approach or leave an object. The purpose is very practical, and the striving for better sight and understanding determines forms. Only later, with the liberation of the camera, is the stage reached where movement gains articulative and interpretive significance. To fully appreciate how this was achieved, one additional distinction must be called to mind. Just as the child's or primitive man's space perception is characterized by the confluence of object and environment—or, in another context, by the syncretic growing together of the "I" and the "not-I"—so, in the sign system of the early cinema, the moving external world appeared as a most unarticulated unit. Only motion itself was enjoyed, without any distinguishing ability as to possible movements of objects and persons, and especially of the camera. On the screen only as much movement was perceived as the spontaneous action of the actors and moving objects produced. The camera did not follow their lives. At best it attempted to record movement in several consecutive time sequences from various distances, which meant only closer or from a more unusual angle. In time, the more cinema broke away from mere reproduction—description and automatic transmission of events—the greater its capacity grew for signification, which was due in no small measure to segmenting, to a conscious articulation of motion. Thus it was possible for thought to gain superiority over the image. In other words, film produced its rich and multilayered meaning by composing movements made of a multitude of equally rich and varied elements. The result was not merely a real photograph of simple physical movements, but the embodiment of a more abstract, sensory, and intellectual "semantic order."

Friedrich Wilhelm Murnau's "drunken camera" was the first to experiment with "subjectifying" the objective camera. But at the time the camera's independence was rather tenuous. Since then we have seen countless "dancing," "flying," "falling," "dreamily floating," and "spinning" cameras. The intention is clear in each case: to penetrate the dynamics of the senses and to identify physically with the mobile interior world of the heroes. But in fact, in all of these solutions we are witnessing only an exchange of roles, of vantage points. Instead of the eyes of the author, it is with those of another chosen person that we look and move about.

The real freedom of space utilization and the realization of its thought-conveying power reached maturity when the various forms of movement struck out on their own in their search for meaning. When the movements of heroes and objects were deliberately separated from those of the camera, the ultimate effect was produced out of the complicated mutual effect of the two movements. We could see this illustrated for the first time in the work of Antonioni about two decades ago. The camera follows someone, lags behind or keeps relentlessly on, not because it is required by the scene's "legibility" or mood, but because the articulate movement of the camera has "poetic" value—it condenses in itself a second, autonomous message. We also see examples of this in Jancsó's often mentioned complicated space formations or in the movement patterns of Glauber Rocha's gory folklore ballets. In these films space becomes a flexible stage imbued with mythical emotions and imagination, a locale stylized in all its aspects and carrying meaning in all its movements; space has become a field in which the imagination may roam free. This can happen because in the rhythms of the camera's movements, in its circling, bending and turning, crossing and surrounding movements, in its slower or faster pace, there lies hidden a poetic ideal, a comprehensive thought independent of the story line.

In *Last Year at Marienbad*, Resnais made his camera the undisputed soloist above all other means of expression. The camera's movement, subordinating everything else to it, was the prime carrier of meaning. As it moved down the corridors, as it lingered gracefully and elegantly over the busy baroque ornamentations or the topiary bushes in the garden, there was no doubt that the camera brought to life a separate universe and established an independent and coherent point of view. What the images by themselves could never have told us—such as questioned certainties and enigmas of the heroes—the camera did manage to convey by casting its cool glance all about, withdrawing, approaching again, amused, then withdrawing again, its expression elegant and mysterious. Its continual strolling, ceaseless mobility, caused unrelenting tension and anticipation: it simply dissolved and eliminated the reality of space. After a while it seemed as if we wandered about in a dream among imaginary sets, and because of this we felt that in this place everything had become relative, any object or event might be replaced by another, one just as fleeting and intangible as any other. Here we truly had an opportunity to experience what it might be like to reject a world in which things and human relationships are fixed, for we were exposed to chance meetings and constantly shifting entities of time and space. The flowing together of the past, present, and future was caused by the dreamlike gliding and magical movements of the camera. Strangely enough, into this work, which had no particular tendency toward irony, it was this mysterious play of the camera that, perhaps unintentionally, did inject a drop of irony, diluting somewhat the authenticity of the aloof heroes.

It has been proved that imaginary space, as depicted by the camera, has knocked down many walls. With easy movements the camera can create and juxtapose space-structures of equal value. It can render perceptible the image of restless, malleable space, in which foreground and background continually shift positions, showing us how inextricably physical and symbolic space-realities are intertwined.

· 3 ·

The Affinities of Film:
The Realm of the Everyday

MIRACLES OF EVERYDAY LIFE

"Film is the discovery of the miraculous in everyday life," Siegfried Kracauer declared over three decades ago. While today it is hard to see anything daring or visionary in this, at the time Kracauer said it, it was both. While the cinema was being tempted by so many artificial and contrived stylistic possibilities, this definition of its relation to life could, at best, be considered an accusation to prove the inferiority and commonness of the film. Very few serious directors were willing to explore the cinema's attraction to the raw and the trivial. Focusing our attention on the inner nature of cinema, we find that true parallels abound between the structure of everyday life and the new medium. The "everydayness" is so inevitable a base that even films that deny it, or treat subjects way above it, must start out from it.

Thanks to the avid curiosity and sensory power of the cinema, we have before us the exhaustive reality of our century, recorded on celluloid. Its habits and fashions, its adventures that have changed our environment, every imprint of its fluctuating taste and temperament; all are contained here, wound on reels and stored in boxes.

A curious museum. For not only the props and the objectified memories of the human comedy are amassed here, but also the action itself as it all happened, in the lively process of change.

Celluloid records so completely that the insignificant, incidental, and superfluous details also appear on the screen, begging for life.

Film takes us along as it penetrates the dense jungle of existence as if to take samples. The inarticulate state of this world, the fusion of so many various impressions, is a peculiarity of everyday perception. In real life, attention is split in many directions at once by a continual deluge of indiscriminate stimuli. It is to counter this ordinary form of experience that the arts and the sciences have forged their weapons, with which we may order, arrange, and logically process the overwhelming amount of impressions. In everyday perception, it seems, classification, selection, and abstraction do not play a demonstrable role; we do not see the order that might rise above the practical, or the chaotic disorderliness.

In this regard it is true that everyday life is the world of the unnoticed, in which existence is mostly deprived of, or removed from, the circumscribed meaning. Routine is a type of mechanical existence tending toward automatism. Hence its comfortable familiarity—which is the sole consolation in the face of the monotony of repetitions. For the numerous, but ultimately repetitive, stimuli become boring; they cease to challenge, and thus reactions grow more and more relaxed, comfortable, and sluggish, creating a peculiar balance between the pulse of the external world and the inner world of the individual. The center, certain and reliable, is always the "I"; everything is measured against it. This is man's most natural and narrowest universe.

Is this then the great gain, the newly conquered continent, film's dowry—all these faded habits, reflexlike functions and vegetative processes; an existence that contains, indiscriminately, the small and the great, the spiritual and the physical, and one that is incapable of clear and definite articulation, mixing and confusing all kinds of values? Values may, indeed, be confused. Qualities? Never. The most interesting, albeit barbaric, characteristic of the film is that it cannot honor the usual hierarchy established between sublime spiritual and more earthly attributes. However, it does give us something in exchange. As opposed to the more lifeless category of abstract differentiation, it gives us the uniqueness and unalterable concreteness of all lifelike traits, and the incomparability of every realized quality. Experiencing the various aspects of nature in such abundance has a near magical effect: we become aware of the singularity of things and realize that the felt occurrence is never to return again. Most probably this is the secret of our attraction to the raw and unformed—where we would meet matter condemned to perish, and the kind that may not be found in any corner of time, and yet we have managed to capture it, for however short a moment, to touch it, hold it as it is delayed for a while on the way to its demise.

EXPANSION

Have we ever seriously considered what inner compulsion led the other arts in our time to admit heterogeneity? Was it an accident that in the "isms" of early twentieth century, experiment after experiment tried to break the old frameworks and do away with homogeneity? The fine arts speak directly of mixed media, but this process of eager integration is known to us from poetry groping its way toward *Fleurs du mal*, celebrating "air, steel, coal, stones," exploding the old supply of metaphors. We have also seen music trying to expand the world of sound beyond the narrow domain of musical instruments by establishing the most universal orchestra possible, making use of any material capable of producing sound. Literature and theater also show expansionist tendencies: raw and processed elements, whether lifted from life or from other forms of art, are appearing in them, well mixed, with increasing frequency.

What is behind this restlessness; what is this urge to annex additional territories; why the dissatisfaction with the limits set by the traditional forms? Is this only a search for expressing the experience of abundance and crowdedness by moving the stimulus-threshold of perception higher and recording blurred and contradictory impressions?

It was no mere exercise in rhetoric when the writers of manifestoes, the first theory-makers of surrealism, spoke of a new ethics. The pursuit of certainty and the impatient longing for palpable authenticity were born of the denial of elegant commonplaces and empty conventions. Like all new methods, this was a moral symbol as well, stating clearly that the existing is already unacceptable. When Picasso got carried away and sewed a dirty shirt onto a canvas, he made a gesture of great import: this picture, at once destroyed and bound tightly together by bits of paper, tattered rags, and old strings, confronted its viewers with an elemental experience. This was not only a visible imprint of a general malaise, of lost harmony, but also a provocation, a defiant curiosity in which the debris of life, disdained and discarded objects, demanded a place on the palette.

Expansion in the arts was unmistakably directed toward unfathomed depths, toward a raw and aggressive existence in which everything given and untouched by nature has a place. The dismal products and throwaway goods of our voracious civilization have triumphantly marched into the closely guarded halls of high art.

An additional source of expansion was the scandalous nature of our instincts, as discovered by Freud. And here, too, a new depth was sounded, for hard on the heels of instincts, the suppressed and discreetly unspoken-of subconscious began rather loudly to justify its right to exist.

Picasso's filthy, torn shirt had become a provocative symbol. Flinging to the wind fine artistic transpositions of representation, it indicated an urgent need to present a coarser reality.

I believe that the film had essentially the same mission. If practical and social circumstances have prevented it from fulfilling this mission completely, it has taken on a good part of the job by bringing closer to us the elements of everyday existence, by conquering the trivial matters of life. It has tried to acquire everything that surrounds us: the bleak and the unadorned, the never-noticed superfluous, the ephemeral and the unworthy of observation. And so the film speaks to us, in Thomas Mann's words, with the unequivocal tones of "the lily and the onion": it has taught us to be fascinated by everyday things.

It may have been Dziga Vertov who first led us out of the cozy workshop of the artisan into the suddenly expanded factories, where working in the shadow of giant machines was at once drudgery and delight. Vertov also took us out to the boulevards and streets ploughed over by streetcar tracks. Walter Ruttmann's *Berlin* showed us not only the "symphony of the big city" but also the dreary, gray reality of getting up at dawn. And then, through countless films, we learned about the joys of Sunday, the stuffy pleasures of pubs, the noisy hilarity of amusement parks, about morose railway stations, and about the man stuck on the conveyor belt of public transportation. . . . Is there anyone among us who would not know precisely what those uniform rows of houses look like in a small English mining town, with the milk bottle and newspaper on each doorstep, or the strapped footwear and quilted jacket of the Russian *muzhik*, or the chattering, sandwich-munching shopgirls spending their lunch hour on Spagna Square?

These are images of a new civilization. This time, however, expansion is not toward some distant land of exotic and rare sights, but rather into that fantastic territory which happens to lie right in our midst: behind the scenes of our everyday life. The film has placed us in a new anthropology, described as the ceremony of tinkering with our gadgets and tools in our familiar environment.

But precisely because it has come so near to what we call our everyday experience, the film has succeeded in recording new phenomena of the changing life-habits of the century. It has captured, with "magic exactness," faces, gestures, and behavior patterns, which previously could not even be named. As if flipping the pages of a huge picture-novel, cinema has generously thrown at our feet all the treasures this side of verbalization and scientific classification, thus confronting us with the changing interactions and relationships between man and nature, man and technology, and, of course, man and man.

CITY LIGHTS—AND SHADOWS

A little man, a pure-hearted tramp, wanders about the asphalt jungle among speeding automobiles, in the shadow of skyscrapers. The swirling multitude sweeps him along, and whenever he is cast out he finds himself up against a wall. In the great crowd he experiences only loneliness and complete neglect. The little man may be bumped, knocked down—nobody cares. Human feeling, this puny flower, blooms only in—or, according to the ways of a bygone age, withdraws into—secluded court-yards. This is how the urbanized image of "modern times," a new civilization's spectacular conquest, appeared in its first classical formulation.

Of course, Chaplin's view was far richer than to touch on only one aspect of the twentieth-century big city. His irony was directed against his own clumsiness as well, and he was more lenient toward the "guilty" environment. This, however, does not alter the fact that in the process of "heredity," only the determinants of the basic conflicts have stayed the same, forming a pattern to be followed when dealing with the big city's antimyth for decades to come.

For, if I may be allowed a brief detour, big-city mythology, obviously, was not born with the cinema. The literature of the end of the last century seems to have taken several steps toward the crystallization of certain situations and types. Everything that was once the privilege of the romantic novel—the spinning of exciting and fateful tales—was now reinterpreted, and the world of shining and fallen heroes, great passion and violence, was brought within arm's reach; it was transferred to the great new stage called the big city. There had been a time when the mysteries of Paris, like the sinful and enchanting secrets of a latter-day Babylon, filled the pages of many an adventure novel. Then, suddenly, a strange "deromanticizing" set in.

Elements of the stories are the same, but the interpretation and packaging change. Everything is drier and more rational. The detective mystery, the cooler game of the thriller, takes over the former haunts of broken hearts and entangled passions. In other words, the role of crime is undergoing a change: it is no longer the diabolical exception, but the inevitable part of everyday life. A more restrained excitement and curiosity, the tension of solving a crossword puzzle, replace the erstwhile full-blooded action fraught with damnation and salvation. The heroes, interestingly enough, appear with the same suggestiveness on both sides: the hunter and the hunted, the victim and the good inspector, who each rule the city with equal wisdom and hidden genius. Each is familiar with every corner of the city; what no one else could possibly know in its entirety, he handles with the greatest self-assurance, treating all the city's vehicles, for example, as so many personal pets. No, this city is no longer a mystery, or a terror-filled night of phantoms, but a happily conquered sober territory, which is comprehensible even in its exaggeration; with all its surprises it is no longer an infernal place.

In its early days the cinema was trying to show us this more familiar face of the city. The German cinema of the twenties and thirties produced a sizable group of films inspired by a romantic anticapitalistic representation of the city. *Die Strasse* (Karl Grüne), *Die Freudlose Gasse* (Georg Wilhelm Pabst), Lang's famous *M*, and von Sternberg's *The Blue Angel* were veritable registries of how crime grows in this soil of the big city. With the help of alluring lights, cafés and bars, and shamelessly tempting streetgirls, these films show the city as a labyrinthine jungle that hides everything and everybody, and in which one can only fall, sink, or be humiliated.

Chaplin at least had some romantic naïveté, some grotesque charm. Later examples took over merely the most ostentatious emblems of the model, turning into cheap symbols human masses, streams of automobiles, lights and noises.

The decisive change occurred with the new wave. I still recall, in 1958, when we first saw Claude Chabrol's *Les Cousins*, how we could hardly pay attention to anything but this newly discovered magic of sparkling liveliness. The city had become the symbol of abundance; it seemed simply inexhaustible. The film made the unrestrainable bustle and the wasteful piling of event upon event our experience. Mesmerized, we were looking at a thousandfold simultaneity; vibration and zest, extravagant and ceaseless movement, in an electrified field of high tension.

How many different faces of the city were beginning to be sketched in for us! Every quarter had a different profile, every district a different atmosphere and aura, changing before us as we moved from fancy apartments to shabby bistros and university cafeterias. We were carried along in the madness of rush hour, rode buses and the Metro, and learned a whole new urban flora and fauna.

There is no reason to assume something mysterious behind all this. We can find very objective explanations for film's successful conquest. And they lie not only in the obvious social and political changes, which made big-city life familiar to millions, but also in the very technical conditions of cinema production.

This was the decade of the widespread acceptance and use of the light, hand-held machine, the completion of the long and arduous process of "the liberation of the camera." With this, the film was at last free of the artificial atmosphere of the stuffy studio and able to roam unhindered anywhere its curiosity took it. After the initial and hesitant probings of neo-realism, natural environment finally came into its own: the street, the apartment, and the real use of nonprofessional performers. Once the camera was free to move about and the photosensitivity of celluloid increased manifoldly, so that no artificial lighting was necessary, the real human milieu, the entire palpable world, became the cinema's hunting ground. The camera could stand still wherever and whenever something interesting was taking place, or follow at will, in time and space, something just unfolding. Painted sets fell away, space expanded. The city, the street, the home and the pub, the railway station and the stairwell, the church, mountains, and rivers now truly and naturally became the objects of cinema; objects in that undisturbed materiality and untouched originality in which God and man created them.

With regard to cinema's mission, thus far we have been able to discuss only its prehistory. On countless occasions since Balázs and Kracauer—and quite justifiably—cinema's greatest accomplishment was expected to be the exploration of the environment and the creation of equality between the Hero and the outside world. But true fulfillment was possible only when the camera could literally be taken into man's hands to record everything within its range.

A little while ago I mentioned how city and cinema seemed to have found each other, as if there existed similarities, affinities, and mutual tendencies that would all but ensure a fruitful encounter between the two. And, indeed, a great number of tumultuous new ways and characteristics of big-city life have developed during the last decades, which only the cinema has succeeded in both recording and sensitively reflecting upon. What has happened to the face of the big city, to the ritual of its customs, in the mirror of the cinema?

STIMULUS DENSITY

The most striking feature of changing city life is the density of stimuli. Nothing characterizes a big city more than its various multitudes: there is a lot of everything in it, and all its corners and holes are filled. One is surrounded by a steady flow of stimuli. Everything is calling, offering itself—merchandise inviting consumers. There is hardly time to orient oneself—focused attention gives way to a peculiar semiawake, semiconscious observation: perceptive consciousness seems to let events pass through it almost with no resistance.

Let us recall Godard again. In a number of his films he chooses the chaos of the swarming big city not as a means but as his subject. He has captured numerous aspects, scenes, flavors, and the rhythm of big-city life. There is, however, one common denominator to all these films. Godard does not reduce these phenomena to good or bad, attractive or repulsive. He probes their unexpected and unpredictable characteristics and wants to test their restiveness. His cuts and isolated segments, therefore, surround us, first of all, with their vitality. We are made to experience the sweeping force of all that happens. We are enwrapped not only in the highly concentrated, often "frazzled" hysteria of everyday life, but also in its repetitious, sometimes intoxicating indifference. Here, opposites face each other constantly: saturation and vacancy, the pale and the ostentatiously colorful, adventure and stultifying boredom. What is Paris, for example, in *Pierrot le Fou*, the city that our heroes want to flee at all cost? Is Paris not all the things mentioned above, and all at the same time? Coldness and constant challenges, racing to make an impression—or perhaps not even that any more, since the piling of sensation upon sensation has already resulted in paralysis. In *Two or Three Things I Know about Her*, although we see a very different Paris, with its monstrous square tenements, the lack of control over one's existence, which flutters unceasingly between extremes, produces the same highly charged tension. Life is feverish activity here, too; it is mechanical, an extremely dehumanizing automatization. To live under the shadow of a superhighway under construction is at once beneficial and destructive. Although the imposing size of things may be called majestic, this does not make them friendly, homely, or in any way warm. Is it any wonder that in this atmosphere only deviation from established norms can hold out the possibility of a last resort? Stealing and prostitution become the only "human" activities in which some semblance of direct relationship can be preserved—as is the case in the works of Godard's model, Brecht.

ANONYMITY

But no matter how dizzying or chaotic the picture of fast-paced and crowded urban life, the city is a system in which existence is organized by a whole network of social, physical, biological, and psychological contacts. As a result of all this, a new type of relationship is born, which is but a series of anonymous contacts. Georg Simmel defines the big city as the domination of the impersonal over the personal, the rule of the objective spirit over the subjective (i.e., the rule of institutionalized culture), which oppresses and withers individuality.

City living has changed our way of life: less and less can a person enjoy the intimacy and warmth of interpersonal relationships. Rather, he lives in the grip of a complex, amorphous organism surrounded by crowds, the physical milieu, and the thick fabric of "metalanguages" serving institutions and indirect communication. This shift of proportions has two consequences: on the one hand, the environment becomes man's real dramatic partner, a challenging and influential antagonist, able to regulate and dictate the course of one's life. On the other hand, personality undergoes a peculiar process of conformity, and only at the cost of the most strenuous efforts and shocks will man be able to assert his own personality, to let his emotions and interests break through the barrier of functional-rational relations and escape the prison of roleplaying.

Cinema's mode of expression, its oft-mentioned impersonal attitude, is decidedly favorable to this new delicate balance. The ineluctable presence of the environment in people's lives is a constant factor on the screen as well. This may allow the film to express city life's heterogeneity with its own characteristic heterogeneity. Things may appear here in their reified form, in their "thingness," appropriate to their real proportions and place in real life. And if in the midst of anonymous social relationships and conditions of stimuli density, speech, as a means of communication, loses most of its impact, this too falls in well with the faculties of cinema. Both in the big city and in the film, whatever is said in words must be necessary information; expressions of emotion and personal feelings are almost immodest and unforgivable. Human contacts do take place, of course, only in a different way: a whole arsenal of nonverbal communication serves to relieve loneliness without the individual's having to give up the reserve and guardedness forced upon him by social rules and his own anonymity. Tiny signals and gestures, a semiosis pressed into refined and visual allusions to fashion and customs, take on the duty of establishing contact. The dominant role in communication, then, is played by means this side of, as well as beyond, verbalization—and need we explain that cinema's language is most eloquent and original precisely in these regions?

THE WEB OF LIFE

Let us take such a sensitive example as Agnès Varda's *Cleo from Five to Seven*. In this deservedly famous film she has attempted to examine how many and what sort of layers are hidden in an arbitrarily cut-out segment of time; what happens to a young woman in Paris one evening, say between five and seven. The film's title indicates that Cleo is the heroine, but if we live through, with her, these two difficult hours of her life, we live not only with her. We also allow her immediate and wider environment and the fluctuating moods of changing events to filter through us as well. We come to know a number of people and things that only cross the scene but still make an impact, for it is the ensemble of people and things that produces that web of life which makes the whole more than an intimate drama of one person, and at the same time more than Simmel's "shapeless sandheap of individuals." Relationships in this film, with all their contingencies, are organically interwoven. Cleo's adventures are exceptionally modest. Her life's radii are also definable: a few people and a few places. She moves about in this limited world carrying her own, similarly limited, universe. What, then, can be considered here real reporting or new information?

What is new is the precise tracing of mutual effects, of absorptions and processing—the mechanism of interactions. Cleo's life-drama—whose distinguishing feature is that man's greatest challenge, the hovering burden of death, is lived through and portrayed in the most prosaic, everyday fashion without any tragic stylization—can be followed in a space that is not artificial, not the abstract field familiar from the stage, i.e., it does not consist simply of the direct contact of people. Only the theater is forced to show the pure persona of its characters (individuals)—shutting out the resistance of live environment. Film returns man to his snail-house, be it a protective or a vulnerable shell. It is to Varda's credit that she does not qualify these factors. She accepts them as given, and, probably as a result of this, she recognizes the friendly and promising aspects as well as the selfish and indifferent ones in the life she shows us.

THE INTERFERENCE OF MOVEMENTS

No matter which episode we look at, a fluidity, the multicolored glittering and the oscillating play of movement and countermovement catch our attention. Cleo buys a hat, Cleo takes a taxi, Cleo leaves for Café Flore—we cannot say our heroine has no "dramatic problem": she is frightened and must get through these couple of hours in order to find out whether she has been marked for early death. And yet who can deny that the "other side" of the action, the impersonal, everyday background, is no less important or interesting than Cleo's personality? Moreover, it is true not only for us, outsiders, but, in a rather convincing manner, for Cleo herself. We might say that this reveals the director's psychological sensitivity: she has understood that the prime result of every dramatic situation is increased intensity, a state of inner stimulation. Sensitivity, in a situation like this, reaches into all areas: this is why Cleo opens up to everything. She recognizes lives, notices people's gestures, almost every ripple in a sea of fleeting events. But in order for this to happen she must be irresistibly surrounded by this live sea of events. Varda has also understood that there is not only simultaneity but also coequality between the "I" and the "not-I," between man and his world. Thus, if she turns the camera "outward," if and when she is checking what the taxi radio is saying in the spring of 1967, what lovers are whispering about in the café, how the magician swallows a frog at the fair, or what games children play in the Bois de Boulogne, she is still concerned with Cleo. She is talking about Cleo, since Cleo is not only what, in her God-given uniqueness, distinguishes her from others; she is also defined by the way she, in her own way, assimilates the outside world. Cleo may pass through life only if she absorbs life's impulses. Even if she later discards most of the superfluous observations and experiences, her figure and character are nothing but this "labor": the way she sees, hears, reflects—the way she accepts and rejects the world.

Is the film indeed so original in this manner of portrayal? A novel, for example, may just as accurately describe all these episodes. Here I must call attention again to the incomparable quantitative richness and qualitative intensity of the cinema. We should also mention the sensuous concreteness with which the film is capable of crowding and making definite and lively all areas of observation and impressions. And because the film does not transmit but records, does not transform but preserves and fixes everything within its line of vision, the sensuous validity of things recorded becomes our direct experience. Cleo's little shudder at the sight of the frog being swallowed is our shudder also, since the rawness of the spectacle has turned the slippery body of the repulsive little animal into a physical stimulus for us—not to mention the barely perceptible movement of swallowing, the flinching face; the reaction of the crowd carries us along, too. Effect-fragments, unfinished events, a multitude of simultaneous stimuli keep the series of images alive. And the heroine slips in and out of them, hide-and-seek fashion, taking on and ignoring their rhythms at the same time. Although her movements have a motor, route, and speed of their own, they constantly change and are modified by her unavoidable contact with other waves of motion; thus the vector of the road she ultimately traverses can be formed only out of the complicated interplay and accumulation of the rhythms of all these interferences.

Just as with the route adjustment of spaceships, linking procedures require corrections. The smaller and greater alterations, however, define and change the rest of the route. Although the ship travels the prescribed route, it could not reach its destination and fulfill its mission were it not capable of deviations, of adjustments to outside conditions.

Cinema's originality in this respect lies only in that it can channel the several streams—varied in nature and coming from many sources—into a single, simultaneous spectacle.

THE CONTINGENT

The big city, as mentioned earlier, is the locale, first of all, of proliferating information, the scene of constant happenings, becomings, and evanescence—all of which makes a sense of anticipation inevitable. Thus the big city has become the distinguished stage of dramatic contingency, where the accidental and the irretrievable are frequent guests—indeed, continually haunting and threatening visitors.

Overexpansion and overcrowding, mutually strengthening and cancelling movements, have created not only unpredictable anxiety but also, paradoxically, the predictability of the unpredictable. If our primary experience is that "everything is possible," it is also a state of readiness and excitement. What is adventure if not this anticipated unknown, a gift thrown at us by chance; or perhaps it is flirting with freedom, the happy illusion that one out-of-the-ordinary step is able to lift us above the humdrum and numbing boredom of the everyday?

Chance meetings are liberating, as can be seen in Cleo's meeting with the soldier, Nana's with the philosopher, and Gelsomina's with the Fool. Of course, people have always met; their fates have gotten entangled throughout the ages. What is new in the cinema is that film turns the very contingency of encounters into an experience by following the slow materialization of objects or people as they are lifted out of the ongoing and amorphous progression of events. As far as Gelsomina is concerned, for example, the Fool is a neutral figure at the beginning. She sees him on the tightrope, looking at him from a distance as he does his daring balancing act. Later, among the circus tents, he is still only a face among many. Then their paths cross, but only to part again shortly thereafter, this time for good. Unexpected meetings always appear on the screen against a total background, extensive and full of movement and intricate happening. We feel that it is not the hero's will, but an unknown cause that is responsible for his appearance. This is also true of his disappearance, as he sinks back into the amorphous stream of events, as do, for instance, the half-witted girl or the frightening riders in Tarkovsky's *Rubljov*.

The accidental appearance of objects underlines our ideas about chance in the cinema even more forcefully. Let us take the famous ship in Antonioni's *Red Desert*. The way it swims into the picture in order to give meaning to an inexpressible mood and then, having accomplished its mission, withdraws, may lend the ship an active dramatic function, making it almost an anthropomorphic participant, but what holds our interest is the ease of movement with which this ship has entered and left the screen, the quiet elegance that has allowed the accidental to appear with all the naturalness of introduction, process, and conclusion.

The new wave welcomed real episodes, mini-events of the street, and freewheeling side trips because it had realized that just by having them it already ensured itself of certain "spicy" elements characteristic of locale and period. And thus, if Jean-Pierre Léaud, for example, in Jerzy Skolimowski's *Le Départ* does nothing but bounce back and forth between girls and cars, he can still be certain that in the course of this loose and impulsive series of incidents there will be an accumulation of thousands of authentic observations and bits of humor and truth that will reveal, at least in some measure, how vague and undefined is the hunger for life of today's teenagers.

THE POWER OF THE ENVIRONMENT

All of the above means together may have been far too meager for another medium, say the novel. Godard's *Masculine-Feminine*, for example, was effective first of all because it succeeded in making tangible and palatable a whole series of environmental factors that shaped the lifestyle of a particular generation. Foremost among these was the framework of big-city life, with its usual but insufferable traffic, countless bistros, and youngsters roaming, always in herdlike groups, between laundromats, white-tiled toilets, and sofas-built-for-three. Within this larger framework, no matter what disorder ruled other human events of lesser or greater importance, the basic texture was attractive, for it recorded real gestures and idiosyncrasies. How could we have distinguished between dramatically designed and accidental events?

Urban development and the shaping of what we call city life have taken place, right before our eyes, with such rapidity in the last few decades that today we may justifiably speak of their decay and disintegration. In the light of these symptoms, Jürgen Habermas's observation seems not in the least exaggerated:

> The problem of the modern big city, in sociological terms, is not to be found in overurbanized life, but rather in that this life has again lost the meaningful characteristics of urban living. The mutual effect of the private and public spheres on each other has been upset. Not because man has become a mass-man, but because the city is increasingly more like an unfathomable jungle in which the individual must withdraw, while the public sphere of activity is reduced to the lowest common denominator determined by tyrannical and ill-organized communication.

What may have been fruitful tensions have now become disruptive and irritating. Neither home nor family can provide the individual with his needed protection and sense of well-being, while public life does not create the kind of community that can ensure conditions of real human contacts.

Many of the often ridiculed "walking films" of the 1960s, after Antonioni, in which the hero's major activity was loafing or roving about, pursued or just unhappy, were born out of this attitude toward life. Monica Vitti's and Jeanne Moreau's languid interest in objects accidentally entering their line of vision, the wearied observation of a lamp post, a sliver of wood floating in a barrel of water, were all reflecting this feeling of "there's no rest in sight," a deep sense of rootlessness.

The big city's heterogeneity, its different lifestyles and varied social and cultural strata, appear on the screen in their most direct naturalism. The film shows us the city's physical, spiritual, and architectural components, the atmosphere and habits of both "upstairs and downstairs," the peculiar folklore of the slums, suburbia, and bohemian quarters, in the selfsame richness and diffusion as we perceive them, in their tumultuous and strange interrelatedness in real life.

Let us consider for a moment the circuitous tracking down of the hero in De Sica's *The Bicycle Thieves*. The marketplace, the workers' quarter, the more selective milieu of the whorehouse, the fortune teller and her apartment, a "better" restaurant—all these by themselves, by dint of their social allusions, informed us of certain tensions building up. Their brief appearance sufficed for us to experience effects that all other mediums would have been able to approach only by extensive and elaborate descriptions.

ROLE PLAYING

In the greatly diversified city life, however, there are numerous fixed and standardized elements: because of the increased importance assumed by institutions, both events and people are becoming more and more formalized and mechanical. One can be only as much as his situation and role will allow. One is either doctor, policeman, bartender, salesman, or go-go dancer, but beyond that: nothing. To step out of the framework, to cross borders, is always scandalous, for we all know full well the "operating procedures" of all the roles, those circumspectly composed "directions for use" that accompany each position to be filled. Cinema not only cannot escape this phenomenon; it rather insists on making it the basic principle of weaving its tales, whose indispensable economy is thus guaranteed by a most complete consensus.

The "ugly singer" in the restaurant—to stay with *The Bicycle Thieves*—fulfills his role as the consoler, his sadness radiating warmth; the indifferent but by no means evil policeman, the wailing mother, and the meddlesome witness all play their roles properly. When the ill-clad laborer ignores class restrictions by entering the high-class restaurant, we cannot but feel that this is an act of disturbing some order, a provocation that will have grave consequences.

Not only movie characters are compelled to follow an unalterable scenario; this is also the fate of outer-directed man. An evaporated personality means that man's autonomy and area of independent actions have shriveled up terribly.

Strict role playing is particularly prevalent in man's relation to his job and to institutions. All of Ermanno Olmi's *Il Posto* (*The Job*) is an exhaustive study of the process of fitting in, of finding one's place through many painful stations, coping with social and psychological conditions. What is the meaning of the Office, Olmi's film asks, and what is the meaning of these impenetrable, almost grotesque roles, and the thick walls separating different tasks? The young boy wanders about the gigantic office building, lost, not understanding anything. But how could he comprehend the pompous, condescendingly amiable psychologist and his convoluted questions, or the cunning zeal of bosses and assistant bosses, or the sad efforts at merrymaking during the office Christmas party? All this strangeness, distasteful elbowing, conceited behavior, and strictness around the boy is, after all, nothing but the solid framework of his future life, his voluntarily chosen bureaucratic existence. What makes Olmi's portrayal valid is that he demonstrates how this monumental and seemingly useless office, despite its haughty and depressing authority, is still the height of aspirations, the temple of dreams for the boy from the slums. Even if he starts in the basement as doorman or messenger, he is in, within the gates, and thus he has taken that all-important first step of his ascent on the mysterious "ladder."

The film builds this peculiar development out of tiny mosaic pieces, out of faces and situations, out of moments of expectations and embarrassment—once again, out of the wealth of its own peculiar ways and means—movements and spectacle whose independent dramatic impact pays off almost effortlessly. The film's findings show nothing extraordinary. Not one turn of events, not one solution can dazzle us with its uniqueness. Instead, the film presents a different experience: authenticity, the kind of incontrovertible conviction that only direct contact can provide. If we wish to have an accurate picture of the Milan of the 1960s, this proud, coolly rich north Italian city in which the curses and blessings of urbanization have found such an impressive expression, Olmi's film might prove to be an exceptionally reliable source. It is a telling and comprehensive document of the Pirelli-type monuments, of the millions of swarming cars of the Fiat kingdom, as well as of human ambitions and aspirations, or norms and limitations, and of stolen or relatively real freedoms.

Olmi's tableau may indeed be characterized as objective—that is why it can demonstrate side by side the attractive and the terrifying, the glittering and the alienating big city. Antonioni, on the other hand, lifts these disparate contents into poetry, into a realm where a uniform emotional tone rules throughout, that of rejection and complaint.

All Antonioni's films from *The Girlfriends* to the *Red Desert* are nothing but a single unbroken confession of hurt, or perhaps only of sadness about the big city as the cruel locale of all human wants, as the desolate landscape of loneliness and homelessness. Antonioni's exclusive neighborhoods reek of desertlike boredom and sterility. Things and objects have senselessly taken over human life; a cool and indifferent anonymity covers everything. Perhaps it is Antonioni who most deeply feels the anxiety of that emotional vacuum which hides behind the loud rationalism of technical civilization. In his films he discloses a complete and consistently negative existence, whose domain has become the cold and rich metropolis, dressed in cement, that has given up its personality. For Antonioni, the cities of Turin, Bologna, and Rome are practically interchangeable. Not only emotions have been stunted by the eclipse of the sun, but also the cities themselves and the meaningful realms of life.

PUBLIC PLACES

Compared to the isolating and atomizing tendencies of the big city, there is an understandable charm attached to so-called public places. The street, for instance, has a unique position just by belonging to everyone and no one all at the same time. The pub or bar, the department store, the bus and the office are to be considered centers of human contact open and accessible to all. These public places have become strange and chaste communal locations, which, because of their heterogeneity, attempt, in some sadly atrophied form and almost as if secretly, to take on the role of the old marketplace. For there is some unnamable complexity in them: a curious sifting ability with which they can, at great speed, group together and separate people gathered at random. Precisely this element of chance, the bizarre ensemble of objects and faceless yet strong-profiled people, is what makes this fabric of dissimilar threads inarticulate and ready to unravel at any moment.

Fellini's heroes, tossed about by hope and despair, rush to places where they might warm up. The world of music halls and circuses may be the answer to a longing for others, for some sort of contact. Having been picked at random by a hypnotist, the woman in *Nights of Cabiria* experiences, for once in her life, the joy of being special. This most personal of feelings is achieved when at last she is surrounded by a community of people, however temporary, and protected by a benevolent anonymity; she has left the role of the prostitute and still she is the cynosure of all eyes. She can be beautiful and the heroine of a miraculously enchanted dream. She is even offered real companionship; for one magic moment she has left loneliness behind.

Restaurants, trains, post offices, and the beach are not simply scenes of certain events; they have acquired an exciting additional quality: they are meeting places that hold out at least the promise that something extraordinary might happen. We still vividly recall the seashore of *A Sunday in August* or the captivating kid on his bottle-collecting rounds on the boardwalk in *The Little Fugitive*. In the latter we are shown, as we follow the little boy, a panoramic view of a modern arena of leisure and public contacts, and how it functions.

The camera penetrates this pliant space, mingling happily with various gatherings, capriciously lingering here or there, then rushing on to other points of interest. And the more it assimilates the rhythm of the bustle, the closer it approaches the true nature of our speeding, pulsating civilization, because movement and the throbbing beat describe this life no less than its stationary spectacles.

INDIFFERENCE

Simmel, in his essay quoted above, seems to detect in the big city's extreme impersonality something paradoxically personal, namely, indifference, which he considers to be the most peculiar mode of adjustment. Reserve, reticence, Simmel maintains, is indispensable to properly balanced human contacts. It is not a lack of reactions but rather a lulling of reactions, an indifference born of some sort of sobriety which ensures a measure of personal freedom not found in any other circumstances.

Simmel also correctly observes that usually this reserve is not disinterest, but rather a quiet counterfeeling that may, at any moment, turn into aggression. Thus, independence teams up with defenselessness, freedom with the most complete loneliness. And below the smooth surface of indifference and tolerance flow streams of emotions and threatening feelings that may break the surface at any time.

We have witnessed in a series of films this treacherously fermenting aggression and nearly irrational hatred as they broke through indifference and detachment. And we have seen them not only as deviant pathological or criminal tendencies, as presented with flawless plasticity in Fritz Lang's *M* and Godard's *Breathless*, but in much more complicated forms. Let us recall the closing series of images of *The Bicycle Thieves*. The rather indifferent pedestrians, led by some inner urge for revenge in something like a lynching mood, throw themselves on the innocent hero and do not let go of him until he is completely humiliated and physically beaten. Where does all this passion, this will to rule over others, this hypocritical sense of justice come from? Not to mention those films in which mass emotions do not stop short of murder, as in *Easy Rider*, where we are made to see each successive wave of hatred until a victim's blood is spilled.

Of course, indifference or treacherous detachment may have more innocent, milder consequences, like tolerance for the irregular. One of the strongest attractions of the big city is that it lets everybody live in his small well-defined place, but it does give elbow room to all comers: hippies, hoboes, incorrigible shirkers of work, the rootless, and those living in close proximity to crime. Have we not seen enough tramps, professional "lifers," loiterers, and modern-day mountebanks on the screen? Many have remarked on the film's predilection for heroes from the ranks of marginal people, on how gratifying their presentation has proved for a more acrid sort of romanticism. In this, too, cinema follows modern urban society: it brings to the fore the ambivalent nature of integration in the big city.

TOO MUCH CONFORMITY

After so many bleak images, let us look at a lighter prospect, which, justifiably, must be treated with a bit of irony: the stumblings of the little man. As is well known, after the Italian neo-realists, it was the Czechs who claimed this territory as their own, laying siege with unerring accuracy to more and more aspects of the little man's bewilderment.

The little man, as he is collectively called, be he a calm train engineer, conscientious fireman, diligent clerk, or sprightly pensioner, is growing in number, taking up more and more space, settling in special sections of the city, creating his own tailor-made life style, which, of course, requires a code of behavior and a "philosophy of life" to match. We all recall the earliest memorable examples of neo-realism: a veritable hall of fame of doormen, court attendants, chattering old café habitués, hefty mothers, fallen chambermaids, and superannuated bathkeepers. Neglected fates locked in sadness; yet they all deserve a measure of humor, a gentle little smile as they do their balancing act on the precariously thin line between clumsiness and an irrepressible talent for survival. No matter how unlucky or fumbling they may be, in their eagerness to please they also manage to remain profitably adaptable; in their humbleness there is also cunning and a validity that will keep them afloat. It is this tradition, and a gibing, but never antagonistic, irony that characterize some of Forman's films. From *Black Peter* to *Taking Off*, all his heroes are marked by gentle and wily feeblemindedness. Most of all—tails between their legs, full of guilt and uncertainty—they wait. They only know that they know nothing of the world. Being out of step, falling behind, and being passed by, despite great sedulity—all this may be called, with Freud, "the new psychopathology of everyday life." Not that we ought to declare these tendencies ill; the label is justified because it describes a real series of symptoms and a general attitude. The anxiety of the outer-directed man, his loss of self, is indeed a felt injury, and the more he feels his independent personality diminish, the more his fear of freedom increases. Since society's values have not become his own inner regulators, he is flustered, he tries to compensate and to adjust, but in his assiduity he inevitably violates a lot of rules. He commits no sin, only makes mistakes, and while these are not tragic, they are serious enough to cause stoppages and breakdowns that force our little man continually to withdraw and panic for being kept somewhere between showing-off and servility.

This behavior is best seen, perhaps, when we deal with the generation gap. It is in this conflict that adults are pathetically compelled to formulate the worn-out lessons of their experience and superfluous wisdom of life and then to bequeath them, like a precious inheritance, to their children. What a useless treasury, what a worthless collection of odds and ends! Witness, for example, the meek, elderly people of *Loves of a Blond* as they try desperately to smooth things over and cover all the traces of the shame that has befallen their little girl—and how they get bogged down in their helplessness, accomplishing nothing. Or recall the mighty efforts of the firemen—those superannuated heroes —as they deal, in blissful incompetence, with the young participants in an annual beauty contest they are organizing. Here, too, every gesture turns into exemplary foolishness and misguidedness. Not even a reported fire can make them use their common sense and give up their compulsive urge to cater to their imagined "norms of behavior."

THE NEED FOR MYTHOLOGY

The hunger for things concrete and banal is not a unique characteristic of the cinema in an age that no longer considers existence a rebellious circumstance but rather accords it special attention. Everywhere in postwar philosophy and the arts the increased interest in direct phenomena and the examination of the processes and modes of life are prevalent, awarding experience full rights and honor. Existence before essence, claimed the new epistemologists; man creates himself. In the light of these views it is understandable that film wished to share in the new interests, emphasizing, first of all, human phenomenological problems, preferring the concrete over the general.

This extensive recording and inventory has inevitably had consequences. It has indeed affected our way of looking at and seeing things as well as our habits of contact with the world. A new element was introduced into the hitherto natural exchange between us and the environment: our vision is film directed; it is influenced by infinite movie memories. Perception and interpretation blend into an indivisible whole, since our comprehension is no longer "virginal"; it no longer contains any innocent parts—anything that could be separated from a predetermined meaning.

"The language of reality, while it was natural, had existed outside our conscience," writes Pasolini, acknowledging the above-mentioned changes. "Now that this language appears to us as a 'written' one, it would be impossible for it not to demand a conscience of its own. The written language of reality will sooner or later alter our concept of it: it will turn our physical contacts with reality into cultural exchanges."

Natural relationships turning into social ones and vice versa is a familiar process: it is the mode of reaction peculiar to myths. Our question is, therefore: What is the nature of this new mythology? Even at first glance it seems rather convincing that the often described conditions of big-city life, everyday existence as dictated by modern civilization, are conducive to the mythologizing process. The encounter then is far from being accidental: increasingly condensed life phenomena, new social agreements, the more and more pervasive new forms of perception, and, by no means least important, the communicative attributes of the film are all headed in a direction where this profane mythology might take root and cinema may enjoy a more accurately definable role.

"We understand new myths less than the old ones," Balzac had already remarked, "even though they are practically eating us up."

In what does the universality of myth lie—what sort of needs bring it to life? Certainly not some vague and irrational interpretation of existence. And not even our wish to conveniently bow before things unknown or unfathomable. Myth is a system that includes the whole network of ideals and values, taboos and rituals, and customs regulating social intercourse. This is why it can serve as a binding force for the community; it can develop and maintain the community's collective consciousness with a compelling force and exemplary will; it prescribes the patterns of behavior. Myth can reach universality, however, only by lifting man out of the confinement of his selfishness. Once, this transcendence was assured by sacral or magical interference. Today, to be sure, a new kind of "divination" or ritual plays the indispensable role of the catalyst. One factor, however, has remained valid throughout the ages: myth attains to the universal by addressing the most personal in the individual. It speaks to the whole man, his entire moral-spiritual being, including his subconscious, causing an aggressively sensuous effect, which is essential for man to be truly touched. Is there a more glorious and fruitful transcendence than the ideal of a fully realized, harmoniously complete man who is able to overcome his own narcissism, enlarge his world, traverse all his "circles of hell," and thus become one with the causes of a wider humanity? Myth is a bridge between the "I" and the "not-I," between the heterogeneous self-conscious and the homogenous image of the world. It is aversion and wish fulfillment; it is the distant and consoling promise of a possible unity and the creation of a sensible and balanced world.

Perhaps now it will be easier to understand modern man's urge to create myths. His life and activities force him into disjointedness and isolation; the channels of contact are barely accessible to him. Myth has, first of all, a cementing, binding function. It must, above all, ensure the community of certain experiences—a collective basis in which norms necessary for action can take hold, according to some sort of agreement—and it must also provide a background where these activities may grow and spread. Myth may help man in other ways, too. It could serve as a pattern for his uncertain and incomplete self-definition; it may be the model for his desired self-portrait. When religious transcendence lost its value, political teleology proved to be too fragile, an easy prey to changing actualities. And so we have our modern myths, somewhat modest and fragmentary, but representing an effective "going beyond" and a comprehensive universality, which may not simply mark out a sober direction, but may also cause man to face the world in an emotionally charged experiential encounter.

Very likely we are dealing here with an odd form of consciousness, but the fact remains that it seems to fulfill an irreplaceable need. Man cannot give up his desire to go beyond himself, and if he can no longer believe in a pure ideology—be it the hereafter or an earthly utopia—he tries to reach completeness indirectly: he proceeds to mythicize his own daily life.

This, therefore, does not mean that myth is the epitome of ignorance, as some vulgarizer once maintained. On the contrary: in myths it is the familiar, the very popular phenomena that receive their desired or feared extension—the appearance of a merciless necessity. Myth lends the severity of law to the fictional image. In other words, it makes whatever exists appear to be axiomatic: reality equals truth, and this tenet cannot be challenged.

Meaning is always broadened and endowed with great sensory power by myths. Daring generalization together with a heightened emotional charge make for an ordering of the world into unambiguous, effectively interpreted basic units. If we recall some of the important early films of the silent era from Griffith to Pudovkin, from Chaplin to Dovzhenko, we realize that their secret lay in their pure and brutal pitting against one another of the forces of good and evil. Mythical consciousness accepts only ultimate truths; this is the basis of its effectiveness. Dismissing all interim levels, myth connects us directly to a lofty universal ideal by speaking and reasoning with us in tones colored by passions and feelings. At the core of these emotion-filled meanings, however, it is not difficult to find the seed of everyday life-events and those existential situations that need explanation and clarification.

Griffith's *Broken Blossoms* and *Birth of a Nation*, in different historical contexts and environments, are both mythical extensions of the same experience, which sees in modern life a threat to old ideals and an era of rising violence. The clash of opposing forces is open and aggressive, and ultimately unaltered even by the obligatory happy ending. The harmony of a romantic ethos informs the Russian films of the 1920s also. *Arsenal* and *The Last Days of St. Petersburg* are examples of how the promise and desired victory of the Revolution is stylized into reality. The strength and consciousness of the workers gain visual and sensory validity in the language of images. Again, good faces evil, with the former's superiority being unquestioned throughout. Even weapons seem to shine differently in the hands of the workers; the ideal of truth is made to appear as absolute truth.

It cannot be claimed, of course, that only the film has created myths of modern life. Both Eliade and Caillois are aware of such rivals of the cinema as cheap escape literature and the "boulevard" theater, which, having left their ritual origins in the obscure past, are still attractive and to some measure meaningful, for they provide the experience of concentrated time. And if this condensed time is without a magical-mythical content, it is still distinctly different from profane time, which it will ultimately conquer—even at the cost of escaping it.

Besides the classical explorers of myths, it is Roland Barthes who has gone farthest in mapping out and illuminating—in bitter and ironic tones—the myths of our everyday life. His reactions stem from the realization that the press, commercials, and the mass media in general, register as natural and self-evident many things that, in essence, are historical. ". . . I resented seeing Nature and History confused at every turn, and I wanted to track down, in the decorative display of *what-goes-without-saying*, the ideological abuse which, in my view, is hidden."[1]

Barthes does not consider myth-making either an innocent or a neutral activity. With the passion of a hunter, he fells famous and popular idols. In the most banal and petty manifestations of life he catches those unforgivable but explainable false oracles and commonplaces with which the modern world so readily and haughtily surrounds itself.

There is more to modern myth, Barthes claims, than simple rhetoric wrapped in an expansive stylization. Its self-justification is somewhat elusive, and its forms are not immediately recognizable. Whether he is poking about photography, travel literature, costumed adventure films, or bellicose journalism, Barthes is looking for a common denominator, a common structure behind the various narcissisitic façades. What Barthes has uncovered is nothing but the awarding of the status of absolute to the unwhole and the ephemeral, shamelessly attributing eternal life to transitory and therefore questionable truths. This is a triumphantly balanced world, ruled by wise harmony, governed with weapons of tautology and pathos. Here everything has its prescribed place; a proud love of order suffers nothing "different." Anything foreign or unusual is quickly assimiliated and reduced to the prevailing level of values. Laws are illuminated by an idyllic happiness; existence is one long holiday, since moderation and common sense spare this world of anything excessive or exaggerated. What is so devilishly cunning in this world is its ability to dismiss with ease everything irregular or undesirable, in such a way as to present pleasant and comforting things not only as given but as of final importance as well. For if this world view, on the one hand, is but a process of homogenizing— mercilessly condemning everything extraordinary or irregular—it also wishes, on the other hand, to upgrade and lift the mediocre above everything: this is the goal of its blissful and soothing effects. Mythicizing touches the banal, for only in this way can the common and everyday acquire special values.

It is here, in the practical-sociological aspects of this world, that film has a role to play. Cinema was the medium that for the first time, thanks to its mass distribution, was able to encompass the whole world and to deliver to it simultaneously the same message. There is no need to elaborate on the unique consequences of this psychosociological phenomenon. We can also see how cinema has developed the optimal technical conditions for world integration.

THE TRIVIAL

What sort of message courses through this infinite network covering the whole world? In a word: the trivial. This has become cinema's true, very own territory. The customs of everyday life, its regulations of ceremonial effects, have acquired visible forms on the celluloid that can be projected on a screen anytime, anyplace. Film has recorded the consolidating process of our civilization, and it has done so while playing a role in the process itself, acting as a catalyst. Not only have we recognized our unconscious-everyday gestures on the screen, but at the same time, because of the film, the patterns of our behavior have become more conscious. Film's repetitions have reminded us of sameness; in its frequently appearing elements we have recognized necessity.

Today it is nothing less than commonplace to speak of cinema's dictatorial role in the world of fashion—how, in our century, it has prescribed in great detail the codes of "good taste" in everything from hairstyles to clothes, proper carriage, and correct accents. We have also seen how some of the more obscure, barely accessible characteristics of our age have turned into anthropological and cultural realities in the finely articulated and distinguished vocabulary of behavior. Film history's first kiss, for example, was not all that innocent. The peculiar combination of elegance and gallant gentility created a model that ultimately turned into an ideal. At the beginning it seemed that the film heavily favored glamor: stars and vamps, sets and lights literally illuminated the gestures of everyday. To dazzle and tempt, attract with luxury, to overwhelm and conquer with spectacle seemed to be the only goal. Then, rather soon, the image got tainted and demands grew coarser; film could happily sink into the common, almost colorless vegetation of existence.

Bars in run-down suburbs, cheap dance halls, windswept docks and lighthouses defined the simple gesture. Jean Gabin's beret and hoarse voice, Michèle Morgan's drenched raincoat were all part and properties of these *Quai des Brumes*. But, at the same time, they also became models in the most physical sense for countless numbers of people. The gait, smiles, inflections, and glances of these stars invited imitation. A whole generation learned ways of flirting and new criteria of "manliness," how to be a "man of few words," cool yet disciplined, etc., from this gallery of temporarily valid patterns of behavior.

EXAGGERATION

Eating, drinking, lovemaking, walking—these are neither strange nor negligible moments of the film, for through these ordinary activities in brings its heroes to life. By integrating these everyday experiences, the film has also helped their development and lent them added meaning. This is how a whole series of gestures, situations, and events have gained the status of symbol. And now we have come close to the very heart of myth. Myth is, undoubtedly, reality raised to the level of celebration, but its festive nature comes from the allowances it makes for exaggeration. In his *Totem and Taboo*, Freud writes: "A festival is an authorized or organized exaggeration. People overstep boundaries not because they feel that some regulation permits it; exaggeration is part of the festivities."

In the film, by means of exaggeration, the simplest activities acquire a festive coloring and become ritualized. As Roger Caillois has said, "ritual is the matrix of myth." If it is true that film raises us out of the everyday in a way that, as Brecht put it, "everything appears to bear a new, unusual stamp," then in this known-unknown, usual-unusual world we may very well meet the new sociopsychological reality of rituals.

Exaggeration concerns not only the course of events, the motivations and effects of human activities. These have always been conveyed by other dramaturgical means. Film has proved its mythmaking ability also by having among its means the magnifying power of exaggeration. This is what we call, following Jakobson, the "poetry of grammar"; in other words, the hallmark of every highly organized construct.

What was said about concrete logic in the previous chapter can now be traced to mythological thinking. Lévi-Strauss points to the real virtue of this mode of cognition in sensory and mutable expressiveness. Referring once again to Roger Caillois, mythological syntax is a system touching on the most diverse levels of human sensitivity, which creates a mutual interference of effects by increasing emotional emphases. There is no myth without "over-determination," he claims, or without the multiplying presence of its various components. This condition, too, is met by the film without the slightest difficulty. Its frequently mentioned ability to render things perceptible pays off: its multifaceted, heterogeneous nature helps capture and surround its spectator from all sides. The film's "hypnotic" effect, frequently condemned in its early days, is part of this unusual function, which is rather similar to mythical experience.

THE RITUALIZATION OF THE EVERYDAY

It was not by accident that at the height of experimentation in the 1920s a large number of important artists turned their attention toward the new, prosaic myths. László Moholy-Nagy, Dziga Vertov, Walter Ruttmann, and Robert Siodmak were independently discovering that face of the big city which had lost nearly all traces of extravagance and romanticism. What they found was the characteristic rhythms of labor and general monotony, the peculiar and at once spectacular symptoms of mass society. The most noteworthy discovery of these "symphonic" approaches was the inner coherence and harmony of the visual themes—with their seemingly accidental existence. The basic structural idea of every film was the same: a search for the cadences of parallels, contrasts, repetitions, and recurring elements. But at the center of each there was only one organizing force, that of labor—labor as socioeconomic necessity, labor as the most direct force among those determining the new ways of life, labor as exploitation and creativity. Clearly related to all this, of course, was the miracle of the machine, the demiurge of this new civilization, its idol and destroyer all in one, as it ubiquitously regulated the flow and rhythm of life.

The hitherto seldom appreciated originality of "big-city films" lay not only in showing and taking over the new physical environment, but, at least as importantly, in describing the new lifestyle as it was being dictated by this new milieu. Beyond the realm of the personal, it was the "ensemble" of movements, their external articulation, rise and fall, and cycles of increasing and decreasing tempo that film had so graphically reflected. Streets, vehicles, meetings, partings are all pulsating parts of a greater web of life; the series of images are feeling their way through a game in which miniscule parts and an invisible whole seem to presume each other's existence. Faces, gestures, and places sink and surface in order to blend, in the end, into the greater flow, the indifferent stream of everyday life.

Subway entrances swallowing up masses of people; giant assembly lines; park benches covered with newspaper; tempting, shapely legs hurrying by; the slow shuffle of old people seeking the sun: all these images are known to us—not from life anymore, but from the movies, where they have become emblems. And as they have become memorable in our consciousness, these images have been transformed into symbols, acquiring a collective value. They are not only reflections but *examples*, gesture-regulating paradigms. They have worked out the ritual of big-city life, making our most common activities consensually accepted and recognized. A process of this sort is based on codification and approval, charged with the consent of "that's how it is," and "that's how it should be."

Now, a few decades later, attention is even more concentrated, focusing more closely on details, looking for a system in more strictly defined areas of life. A series of documentaries, British precision, and sociological sensitivity lead us to unknown territories. Just one example will demonstrate a change not in interest but in the intensity of approach: *Every Day Except Christmas*.

"This is how the big city awakens at dawn, every day except Christmas," says Karel Reisz's film, and in front of his camera we see the most rigorously disciplined, ritualistically executed, and exhausting labor of the market-hall. Definite time and space delimit all activities here: each and every day the same amount of produce must be carried in and arranged in architectural piles. The twenty-minute film highlights the order, repetitive nature, and major stations of this labor, which takes several hours. The emphasis thus gained lends the most common labor of porters and carriers some form, a ritual prescription. And what ultimately emerges from this short film is nothing less than a metaphor of human struggle, an "abbreviated drama" of effort and ambition, a will to succeed. In the early morning preparation of the market-hall we suddenly feel the conflict of all preparations: the contradiction that is always present between deed and realization, vigorous activity and reaching one's goal. Labor is palpable as we watch the concerted effort; we see it as a trial to be passed in order to succeed. We are also given a chance to experience the drama of completion: we have before us marvelous towers and shapely piles of apples and vegetables, fascinating mountains of meat—a truly magnificent panorama, a most colorful exhibition. But as we delight in the sight's artistry, it is impossible not to think of the absurdity of this spectacular display: it is but the ephemeral beauty of a few short hours, which will be destroyed by its own destiny so that the entire cycle may begin anew the following morning.

Is this then a paradigm of existence, an archetypal situation? Whether or not it is sacrilegious to mention these concepts in connection with cabbage, sweat, lugging sacks, or cheap bars, the fact remains that in the cinema the most profane human activities and everyday misery appear as extraordinary and comprehensive experiences, which, charged with the emotional content of ceremonies, present to us the malevolence as well as the benevolent pathos of labor.

The example of Reisz's film is purposely modest. I picked it precisely for this reason—to show the compelling mythicizing nature of the film, the ambiguity of presenting banality containing the metaphor. And further, to verify film's ability to lend a challenging quality to everyday phenomena with its raw emphases and articulation of recurring rhythms, to address us both emotionally and intellectually.

ARCHAIZING NATURAL EXISTENCE

As opposed to the sophisticated neuroses of the big city and our experience of accelerated time, there frequently appears on the screen a way of life that seems warmer, closer to nature. Its chief values are safety and permanence; here, not a partial rationalism but a sober order, honest and open, rules people's lives. Everything that must happen does happen—hence the unshakable experience of continuity and certainty.

It is not by chance that this image is most frequently that of the village, with its elementary forms of existence that guard old customs, moral laws, and an easygoing pace. Its peace and serenity appear as a propitiation of the gods, its identification with nature as a pious return to a lost paradise.

In Varda's first film, *La Pointe courte*, for example, the village serves as a contrast to other modes of life, a secure basis from which one may gain strength and learn wisdom. The sensitive depiction of this life is still attractive today, but the unconditional exaltation of its values seems rather naïve.

Varda was evidently moved by the obvious purity of this tiny, out-of-the-way fishing village, which offered itself too easily as a tower of strength when compared to the tortured and complicated life of urban intellectuals. Perhaps this is why the empty, winding country lane, the fluttering sheets on the line, the chorus of mourning women around the dead child's coffin, and the dazzling, blindingly white and gay water festival seem so beautiful. And while this documentary part is all gentle and supple motion, following the accents and pulse of an even-tempered life, the other strand in the fabric is nothing but tense motionlessness. This is achieved through protracted, stimulating series of medium shots and close-ups conveying the uselessness of self-torment and introversion. The stylistic approach, composed of crossings and emphasized by inversions, succeeds in accentuating the relationship between the two modes of life. Rest and motion, documentarylike and almost calligraphically picturesque frames together serve the film's content powerfully. Nothing would have been easier than to present the life of the village as peaceful and dignified and the impatient heroes' calvary as restless, exciting, and turbulent. But the surplus of content, thanks to inversion, speaks to us more plastically than any other explicit or conventional method and satisfies the demands of mythicizing with unusual suggestiveness.

East European film is rich in examples that show the peasant world as the unique locale of permanent human values. These societies, slow-moving and settled in agriculture too long, have naturally clung to traditional values of morality and customs, and in the changing circumstances have returned, as to a safe haven, to their archaic-romantic ethos.

One of the most memorable of these films is Ferenc Kósa's prize-winning *Tizezer nap* (*Ten Thousand Suns*), which amalgamates all the motifs of this neoromantic mythology. It places in the center of its world the nearly mystical bond between man and nature, going far beyond man's sociological or historical definition. Man, according to this concept, is an organic part of nature, a silent and loyal extension of it. His labor and life are regulated by the cycle of the seasons. There is nothing besides what heaven and earth have given; man's duty is to serve. Does history storm over his head? Do fat and lean years alternate? Are man's ranks decimated by war? Is his family scattered by tyranny? No matter—the earth is eternal, uniquely permanent. It provides bread and life; it is unstoppable; its cycles are forever ending and beginning.

This immense power—laws beyond chance and accidents—can be nothing but beautiful, divinely beautiful. For this reason, everything that creates itself naturally is, first of all, beautiful. It has dignity and noble proportions. Man fits into nature as a modest little dot, a dwarfed subordinate.

Kósa's film has become the historical epos of the Hungarian soil. By composing into images its *puszta* (steppe) and rivers, rare forests and destitute villages, it has also sung the song of the lumbering, yoke-bearing peasant in archaizing language and poetic tones no less lofty than those of the great heroic epics of the past. Each episode is an historical cross-section, a parable and a generalization. We witness here the creation of an interesting method of meditative description, for the entire material is defined by a structure that obeys, primarily, the rules of beauty. Thought surfaces through the order and artistic composition of objects, since here every object is a carrier of history by being the most concentrated folkloric imprint of the creative ability of the people.

Archaizing gestures of this magnitude have appeared elsewhere perhaps only in some Greek films, such as Dassin's famous mystery play, *He Who Must Die*, which even in its genre has adopted the mythical-ritual form of the Passion. It is true, however, that here the landscape and other prehistoric elements of nature are cruder and more cruel than in the Hungarian film just discussed. The aesthetic will is looking for form not so much in pictorial calligraphy as in an historical-mythical reporting: gestures, human groupings, the behavior of the chorus of country folk, and a bleak, raw background must play the obligatory mythical roles. The ominous atmosphere of the tragedy is ensured by sharp black-and-white contrasts and the presence of an inexorable, severe environment.

LYRICISM OF LANDSCAPE PAINTING

And, finally, we may include here the great landscape artists of the cinema. Dovzhenko and the very different John Ford were both not only obsessed lovers but also creative lyricists of nature and landscapes. Wide open spaces were nearly the exclusive sources of their lyric vocabulary. Dovzhenko, for example, could bring within arm's reach the living, breathing reality of the soil, trees, and fruit with unique gentleness and sensuality. His plump apples and oily-skinned leaves beaten by heavy rain are charged with strong eroticism. No one has managed to present the thrilling power of a summer night or a hypnotic moon with such expansiveness. Finite proportions and alternating horizons of near and far open up new sobering vistas. Dovzhenko seems to understand the gentleness and even the serenity of death; he is able and daring enough to surround it with so much and such unusual beauty.

Of the new generation of directors, perhaps only Bo Widerberg is related, distantly, to Dovhzenko. Widerberg consistently places his warm and attractive heroes into a matching milieu. The need for beauty here does not lead to ceremoniousness. It is rather colored by a uniform "douceur": the gentleness and friendly countenance of mountains, forests, and lights. They surround man like friendly, accepting, and protective partners—like allies. Their mildness radiates peace. All this, of course, serves as a contrast to the cruelty of the world. The unspoilable harmony of nature gains special meaning by being placed opposite the world's distortions and murderous laws. Nature here wants to remind us that another order, that of beauty, also exists. These are the captivating images in *Elvira Madigan*, *Adalen*, and *Joe Hill*. All of Widerberg's lyrical tendencies are concentrated here, evoking the landscape of the impressionists—humid, bright, appearing from behind curtains of fog or clouds. Each shade or hue, each spot of light, and the intimate harmony of colors speak more eloquently than any figurative composition could. Widerberg's experiments belong among those few convincing ones that have proved that the pictorial quality of the film can be an artistic structural principle of matter in motion.

However, on closer inspection, it becomes clear that at the bottom of this view lie mythicizing simplification and romantic archaization. For nature is far from being the embodiment of Beauty. Nature realizes what is required by the laws of life, and that is more than noble grandeur or an eye-pleasing variety of events. Nature is no less a struggling organism than our man-made social existence, and therefore it is not surprising to find clashes, battles and death, destruction and devastation among its elements. The overly spectacular confrontation between nature and society is always a romantic act, and while there is no need to completely underestimate its poetic virtues, we must question its proclaimed universal truth. This is all the more necessary, for in this division, nature versus society, the outside world is given a much too undifferentiated, simplified role: it is a coarse, dog-eat-dog world. The critical attitude is perhaps too eager to find a solution in some idyllic return whose suspicious charm is not that difficult to doubt. Maybe this explains why, in the world of the film, we hardly come across any followers of this attitude. The true territory of myth has remained the big city, the jungle of the metropolis.

· 4 ·

The Language of Immediacy: Metonymic Writing

Film, then, is not poetry—it is more and less than that: it is everyday mythology, and not only because of its subject matter and function but also because of its mode of writing. Its language is prosaic, one that must cull all its wealth from its poverty and seeming plainness. In this language banality is placed under the microscope.

Let us take an irreducibly simple example, the opening shots of Cassavetes' *Shadows*. A young man wants to cross the street. In order to do that he must negotiate bumper-to-bumper traffic. The way he takes off, zigzags, is brought to a halt, and then, with renewed determination, starts again seems to reflect the most banal and basic situation of our physical existence.

The exact evocation of one event, however, creates a halo around the meaning of the images. Why is it that we do not feel these images to be a simple recording of an occurrence but consider it a general statement? The boy crosses the street, moves, uses his hands, and vacillates between determination and retreat as if he were struggling across an overflowing river. The unbroken line of cars rumbles before him exactly like a river, and as such it surrounds him, threatening to swallow him up. The upheld hand, like that of a drowning man, is trying to signal for help. And as the various images follow each other, as one fragment answers the call of the one before it, finally a dim light of a metaphor enters our consciousness, and an abstract meaning takes shape.

This invisible and reserved articulation is perhaps the most particularly poetic method of the film. Jakobson calls it metonymic, for it achieves its added significance by situating its elements in each other's "neighborhood," by the simple succession of various combinations. It finds its most meaningful centers of reality formations capable of establishing contact among themselves in the "horizontal" stream of natural progression. Contiguity condenses and amplifies energies, lead-ing to a particular discharge of this newly created tension. It is only a question of emphasis how these various energized areas become ef-fective, or how, through stress (synechdoche) a concentration can be created in which the parts lose their former unique concreteness.

If in the above example of *Shadows* we recognize a sweeping cur-rent, then we understand that the subject is not the motion and tempo of individual cars, but tempo and movement in general. For the emphasis is not only on an intensified approach, on magnification, but also on demarcation, therefore on isolation, on a radical cutting off from con-crete circumstances.

And further, emphasis is not only a spatial operation but a temporal one as well, allowing us to perceive the author's intention.

This elaboration is present in the most banal and commonplace scenes, such as the one quoted above. The camera lingers over some details, ignores others, suspends time, and all these factors help the process of abstraction and intellectual associations that the images provoke.

What we see is neither a simple description nor a slice of life, but a communication of symbolic value—however familiar.

But just how familiar or unfamiliar is this communication? It is familiar as a superficial appearance, as experience so often lived through that it is no longer noticed. But the moment it is broken down into its elements, the most banal experience becomes unfamiliar. What is un-familiar is the patient observation and the components of the process that cannot be seen in the whole: structure as opposed to form, conflict as opposed to states of calm and serenity; in a word, laws as opposed to disorderly phenomena.

What is unusual, rather, is that this "law" comes dressed in a loose garb with very few festive emblems. Here, too, we are dealing with a live image that stands only for itself, carries only its own content. Sym-bolic expression is rooted in natural expression; still, the sense created by objects and everyday phenomena does not sufficiently cover the received meaning. In context, this meaning becomes richer and of wider ramification. No matter how closely it guards its own life, every characteristic of the concrete reality of physical events, as well as the dynamics and even the proportions of those events, is bound up with sensations of an anthropological reality. And thus, because of the author's will, conception, world view, and distorting personal touch, there is another, more distant meaning also present: signification, as understood by the French—at once sense and significance.

The combined effect of immediate reality and its transcendence may be well observed in De Seta's *Banditi à Orgosolo*. The obduracy of passion is shown us through the stations of the fateful interdependence of flock and shepherd, self-defense, escape, revenge, and fatal justice. Every moment is tied to facts of the physical world. The shepherd drives his flock across hills and dales to reach water and to ensure a safe and ample pasture for them. And yet, these natural reasons gradually lose more and more of their significance, and the organizing power of the form seems to be making room for a more comprehensive content. Our first cue is repetition and refrainlike recurrences. The harassed and increasingly hopeless rush is punctuated by necessary and cruelly similar stops: death is decimating the animals. Its repeated appearance causes not only a natural division but, alluding to previous appearances, an emotional accumulation as well. Death's oppressive power is stressed by two stylistic means: a plastic and a rhythmic-structural principle. First, it is not the usual close-ups but just their opposite, the long shots, that are called upon to provide the needed generalization. In the suddenly widened scene we can see the long row of carcasses in all its woeful magnitude. Distance at once opens up not only space but metaphysical perspective, too. And repetition, as always when handled well, reveals not only sameness but also changes; it includes the variations also, since the continual modification of the situation is the spectacle of loss, the source of tension. The rhythmic composition takes shape in the acceleration of time. The shortened intervals, the more frequently arriving blows, drive home the inevitability of fate. The expanded level of meaning thus lifts the series of images to the level of necessity; it lends them the gravity of laws.

We are now facing the true ambivalence of filmic mythicizing. While physical reality is unquestionably present on the screen at all times, its total effectiveness can be achieved only by dimming this reality's meaning, so that on this reduced field, now taken over by newly released energies, it can provide further interpretive possibilities for our imagination.

This is a paradoxical gesture, for it reduces and widens, removes and brings closer all at the same time. Still, despite the many dualities involved, the final result is the finding of the right, gilded frame. For myth always tries to bestow a drop of eternity on its stolen or borrowed objects. With the pathos of unalterability it wants to gild the figures and situations of everyday existence.

RITENUTO AND ENDGAME

There is a very large group of films that consistently and purposefully rely on the tensions of everyday events and their mode of unfolding. The structures of these films are characterized by an exceptionally patient biding of time, a relaxed, yet increasingly more intriguing, retardation of final occurrences. With ominous accumulation, and with a nearly indifferent attitude, they juxtapose their episodes. What we see everywhere is nothing but stressed trivia, the usual ceremonies of everyday life—as in Kazan's *Visitors, Easy Rider*, Fleischmann's *Jagdszenen*, or, the most mature of them all, Ferreri's *Dillinger é morto*—until suddenly, anticipated or not, with one turn there is an explosion, and from below the calm surface, extreme emotions and violence are unleashed.

The delayed open clash, however, is not at all a dramaturgical device. The carefully analyzed events possess a structure that breaks up only after long and well-disciplined restraints. This is how structure can throw light on the latent nature of aggression, by hiding long behind the indifference of events, with a treacherous disinterestedness and unnamable threat. In *Easy Rider*, for example, we have no clue as to the final destination of the heroes, rushing and speeding, restlessly roaming about the country. While we feel that their destiny will not be "good," in just what form the "bad" will swoop down on them we cannot guess by watching the epic unfolding of their story. The unpredictable and rationally unexplainable is part of the phenomenon presented to us. This is why it is inevitable that the fatal shot be fired by unknown persons, faceless and personally unmotivated killers.

Similarly, Kazan's visitors, disciplined and well-behaved, sit politely through the long, seemingly uneventful dinner. They make all the proper responses to their host's hospitality, and then, as if on a secret signal, they set about their hideous mission. Violence is carried out with the same cool and matter-of-fact fashion as were the little ceremonies of the dinner: without emotions and, one is tempted to say, elegantly.

I believe that only in this way, in these unusual proportions, can the desired thought be expressed. To say something new of the current face of violence, to grasp its virulent naturalness, its frightening and unbridled freedom, we must have a precise and detailed presentation of how securely it is embedded in our everyday life.

The same phenomenon is approached from a different angle by Marco Ferreri's masterpiece, *Dillinger é morto*. At the center of his investigation we find a study of boredom and aimlessness. By comparison, Antonioni's pioneer experiments seem like exercises in vague and lyric emotionalism. Nothing and nonevents are stretched to near infinity in Ferreri's detailed descriptions. Every moment he presents what is *not*, photographs what is *not* worth noting. And he does this with such devotion and scientific precision that the method itself becomes very illuminating: the content is but the ironic and philosophic expounding of this absurdity.

Ferreri seems to be asking the following question: What can the average bourgeois-intellectual do—surrounded by his pretty wife and reasonably attractive maid in a well-equipped apartment, complete with exotic potted plants and a home-movie projector—in order to survive when he returns home, full of his job's monotony and the world's news, and must still go through a considerable amount of living? The answer: all he can do is consume time. This is what Ferreri records with the impersonal objectivity of laboratory procedures: these hopeless attempts to kill time, bogged down in a million tiny physical activities.

Ferreri's method can perhaps be compared to that of the *nouveau roman*, which, because of the disappearance of personality, has transformed structure by putting more and more emphasis on objects. In the new novel, too, the autonomy of the outside world rules, its independence outweighing that of the individual. Thus man's sphere of movement is drastically reduced, and his activities grow more impotent and introverted. It is interesting that when the novel made use of this realization, it had borrowed, and not by accident, from the cinema, for above all it was the film that could project before us in all its bleak nakedness a world robbed of human subjectivity. Now Ferreri "re-borrows" the method in order to show us things and objects just as they are, as realities standing for themselves. They have only objective materiality; no feelings are lurking in them. The fate of things is simply to be present. Their function is in their presence, whose goal is to divest them, as consistently as possible, of all the conventional meanings stuck to them in the course of time. At first sight this may appear to be sheer destruction: as if this stripping—as Barthes has often complained—would also remove live contacts, depriving objects of the metaphysical dimensions that analogies usually provide. But is this really what is happening? Not if we consider that this meaninglessness is only an illusion, or rather a graphic expression of a paradox we know well, namely that everyday things and objects have indeed lost their deep human meanings. This negative significance, this missing layer, is what the film can make visible when it descends into the object-world's unintelligible jungle and presents it to us for what it really is: chaos, indifference, and dreary subsistence; it is an empty existence, or, if you will, a nonexistence.

But let us return to the concrete stylistic maneuvers of *Dillinger é morto*. If in the long series of images all we see is how our bored hero potters about the kitchen, pours honey over the back of his mistress, hoping to stir up some excitement, or makes preparations to show a film, only to shove the projector disgustedly aside, and then suddenly paints little red dots on an unexpectedly found revolver—all these trivial, meaningless motions and numerous objects still mean something. They are tropes, or, more precisely, "a similarity built on contiguity," a metonymy that produces an invisible truth by arranging things in order. This is carried to the point where the destructive boredom turns into real destruction, and the loaded weapon playfully (?) or seriously (?) goes off, completing the senseless action in the only sensible way.

Fleischmann works with a similar technique, leisurely placing brick upon brick, lining up slice-of-life episodes from here and there in an apparently loosely organized, almost arbitrary fashion. He heightens his effect by the documentary naturalism of his heroes' environment. The burly peasants of Lower Bavaria and the inns and barns of the village create an increasingly depressing atmosphere. Treachery, again, rises before our eyes, and a hunger for destruction seems to be growing. And then everything rushes headlong toward disaster, with the speed of merciless fate. Defenselessness and reprobation not only make the hero vulnerable; they also drive him to murder, for violence always sets off a chain reaction that escalates until a complete catastrophe is provoked.

THE ROLE OF THE DOCUMENTARY

It is not by chance that Fleischmann made his film in a natural environment and mostly with nonprofessional actors. Other representatives of this method work with similar inspiration and also display a high degree of objectivity. Along with others, Fleischmann has recognized his own vital medium in those regions of life which have so long been exiled by the arts. The more impersonal the scrutiny, the greater the discoveries will be, for a real series of cross-sections broken down to their minutest elements always reveals functioning organisms—both in their space-time structures and in their situational context. Each of these cross-sections is a transit station of an infinite process of movement. No contrived dramatic turns could create tensions to match the kind that can be gained by catching in the act the "just happening," "just now moving" unconscious reactions and the endless manifestations of chance's unpredictability. The boringly slow advance of action, for these reasons, gets filled up with the excitement of anticipation, sharpening our attention and increasing our participation. We find ourselves searching among the components of the phenomenon before us: which one promises change, where will the continuation of this moment lead us? A noisy pub scene, for example, can remain a trite cliché if left abstract and general. But as soon as we linger, in a character-revealing proximity, over the faces, we become witnesses to gestures as they are born, and suddenly we are struck by the novelty of the unpredictable. We have entered a different world. From the conventions of an artificially created environment we have moved into the undisturbed and unsurveyable one of reality.

The role of the documentary has grown noticeably in the last decades. It has spread in all directions, penetrating even the protected areas of fiction. The borders have become flexible, often blurred. Story has gotten mixed in with direct unprepared recording on the one hand, and, on the other, fictional and directed episodes have slipped into documentaries. As always, this cross-grafting has produced surprising results, with an added interest arising from the undefinability of the new genre. While documentary had the impact of life's cunning, the sort of inventiveness "chess-dramaturgy" had long lost, fiction could still offer an organizing coherence and well-defined viewpoint. Both the raw material and the framework—a kind of reduced fiction—openly acknowledged a sober distance inherent in approaching a subject. Ambition took the road of intensification; advances were sought and made not in the imagination but in the very depths of our direct environment. It is understandable that in this strategy each fact appeared to be of equal value, adding up to a new continent to be conquered.

A classic example is Visconti's *La terra trema*, whose elementary suggestiveness has rarely been equaled. It seems certain that the austere power of the film is inseparable from its creator's rigorous convictions; it is impossible not to feel the moral seriousness of the work. The description of a fishing village's obstinate strike has a pathos that comes from a will to exhort, to inform of a new social truth. No matter what the center of our attention is—an object or human faces—it is always filled with the same emotion, lending the film a relentless unity. As if carved out of the same block, each frame is permeated with the same passionate truth. Human speech, just as the voices themselves, the movements of men and women, just as their landscape, are all powerful, bleak, and pared down, unfamiliar with softness. The storm of the sea becomes, almost inevitably, the basic metaphor of these simple lives.

Paulo Vittorio Taviani's *Mio padre, padrone* reaches back, thirty years after Visconti, to the same tradition to tell the story of an illiterate Sicilian boy. The real battlefield here is the environment. The boy's fate is one unbroken war: fighting with his cruel father, but no less with the desolate land, struggling with the sheep straying onto the rocky mountainside, and combating an unbearable personal isolation. Thus the simplest image of the film is metaphoric: it not only stands for itself but signifies an insufferable, condemned life. Scorching sun and bone-chilling cold nights, fear of the dark all become palpable experiences. Only the real landscape's natural presence, a ditch in which the boy masturbates, the proximity of the animals, and the sound of a harmonica in the distance, could so authentically convey the pain of confinement and longing. We feel that in the monotony of life-fragments set in a row there is no planned dramaturgy, for it is the shapelessness that provides the most distressing and authentic impression.

It is Francesco Rosi who has worked out in a series of films the possibilities of blending fiction and documentary. In *Hands over the City* he already put great emphasis on direct presentation of quoted facts; his truly original approach, however, was realized in *The Mattei Affair*. The unusual characteristic of this new genre is that beside the necessarily journalistic nature of the documentary, traces of a Brechtian theatrical process can also be seen in it: constant replays and sudden caesuras lend the material the potential energy of a commentary. This double handling of the material increases the objectivity of the film's tone: commentary and documentary represent, in different ways, the "alienation effect" of intellectual interpretation, arrangement, and annotation, while at the same time ensuring the logical articulation of thought.

ANTIFILM

"Europe is haunted by a specter, the phantom of antifilm," the cry was heard many years ago. Well, the phantom did do some damage but was unable to shake the world to its foundation. However, it has brought to the surface a number of constructive elements as well.

The first step was the crushing of the story. There had been numerous precedents for this, but now the way it was done and the new integration it led to proved to be interesting. We may sum it all up very briefly thus: the principle of montage was replaced by the method of collage; the earlier narrative and logical discontinuity was exchanged for a totally heterogeneous texture. Beyond the breaking down of chronology, the selection of all the components became antitraditionally expansive: the camera became omnivorous. It now appears to have gobbled up everything: fiction, documents, notes, story fragments, playful commentaries, and animated parodies—absolutely everything. At first, mistakenly, it was called an essayistic method, but in truth all that happened was that the one-dimensionality of depiction was relegated to the background in favor of a multidimensional reflection; alongside the sketchy presentation of the story and various approaches and interpretations, a second and a third dimension were added.

The most illustrative example of this is perhaps Makavejev's *Love Affair*. The film opens with a sexologist's treatise, whose seriousness we have no reason to doubt. Still, the peculiar tone and overly scientific approach immediately cause associations of another, more ironic meaning. And then begins the astonishingly insignificant story: the love affair of a telephone operator and a rat exterminator. Suddenly obscurities and dark spots intrude; little fragments flash up: a dissecting room with the unrecognizable corpse of a young woman, a necklace, and underwear held as material evidence. And then another dry, scientific lecture, this time in the jargon of criminology, but it is so detailed that we cannot make out the case itself. In the meantime, the affair proceeds on its banal way: cake-baking, lovemaking, waking together in bed, turning in together at night, etc. And then comes another layer: the events in the life of the little town as they, too, peek into the story: preparations for a May Day demonstration, emblems of a forcibly politicized public life, all interestingly linked with television programs of similar inspirations.

Were we to analyze the structure of these layers, we might distinguish two main axes. The first would be a horizontal one proceeding on the path of regular melodrama, where event follows event: love, jealousy, infidelity, and death. But this progression is continually up against a counterpoint of various retarding interruptions: scientific, criminological, and historical viewpoints offering themselves as explanations. This is the second axis, a vertical one, for it is consciously independent of the dimension of time, and it keeps contact not only with the story but also with the several layers of alternating hierarchical positions. The result is a peculiar relativity: the harmony is nothing but some sort of mocking and playful irony.

How charmingly limited each partial explanation becomes! The more expansive they try to be, each in its own way, the more obvious it is that the effort is greater than the result, for the rights of the other explanations cannot be denied either. And thus, the multitude of motivations turns into a huge question about the irony of motivations. One certainty remains—that of facts, which speak of the secret nature of human emotions, or, if you like, of the ignorance with which we view—scared and confused, humble and haughty—the unpredictable.

Makavejev's method is far more complex than the apparently irregular ways of Godard's films. In the former's work the commentaries mentioned above embody real and functioning explanations of existence, and their mutual allusions and interdependence give them a completeness—I emphasize again, an ironic completeness. They speak of the ignorance of knowledge, of the relativity of our efforts, but without reaching a stage of total denial or resignation. In the very core there is something unspoilable: the simple vegetative quality of everyday life, its passionate yet grotesque intensity born of melodrama. In this light, the trivial is also meaningful, for death endows the most modest things with a serious tone. On the other hand, the serious can hope only for a fallible end: competence and scientific ambition are surpassed only by obtuseness. Ultimately, all these elements create a puzzlelike master structure, in which forward motion is realized through continual interferences and countermovements. And we understand that the passing of time is ceaselessly charged with retrospective allusions, since whatever is unfolding before us is only an irreparable memory of the past.

Makavejev's film is a precise illustration of a wry witticism concerning deep shallows and shallow depths. It turns traditional values upside down, yet keeps them together and makes them reflect one another— and what is this, if not the reconstruction of the groping nature of our thinking, the uncertain pendulum swing of the inquiring mind? The cleverness of the method lies in that it shows how everything is realized by the grace of contact and its unexpected gestures. Thought lives only in the oscillating severance and reestablishment of ties, in dark spots and illuminating fragments. And thus the common, the unconscious, acquires a secret meaning and real depth, while the sophisticated and super-brainy is seen as comic and transparent. Still, they are complementary and belong together, and, just as in ballet, their shifting positions are never final but are rather the very essence of the event at the moment.

POSTER AND COMMENTARY

Makavejev's strengths are his dexterity in balancing complex elements and his simultaneous application of tenderness and humor. Other iconoclastic film makers are noted for attacking traditional forms with the open use of political journalism. This is the case in Godard's latest films, *Ici et ailleurs* and *Comment ca va*, which are debatable continuations of the much earlier *One Plus One*.

There is no reason to doubt the validity of a gesture. Everything is possible if it can prove itself to be valid. That is why the lack of proof is due, first of all, to the thought and not to the method. Even the enlarged role of verbal language is understandable and forgivable, because language here demands a place for itself not only as the direct conveyor of thought but also as a symptom of a sick culture: ossified, dead clichés and word-oceans flood our lives without illuminating them. The various quotations automatically become ironic; their apodictic and aphoristic nature also expresses their sloganlike comic abstraction. Still, at least with Godard, verbal truths have a special place, since they are the most unambiguous and direct means of information.

In these consciously simplified political tractates the customary hierarchy of film expression is reversed: language's retaking of pride of place is part of the provocation. The film wishes to get as far as possible from aesthetics and to avoid calligraphy just as much as the sins of bourgeois culture. Instead it broadcasts slogans in its own uncultured tongue, spectacularly denying the lies glorifying beauty with the cracked and loudly multifaceted technique of the collage. In its external appearance it recalls the newspaper: cartoons, boldface headlines, aggressive information, and deliberately didactic language—all admitting only the one-dimensional truth of an ideology. Its arguments and allusions sound the same way: instructive "engraving" and arrogant repetition of the message. There is no bridge between the intellectual and the sensuous communication.

This concept equalizes everything at the level of building blocks. *Saint Juste* and *Mein Kampf* are both part of the same stock of prefabricated pieces that can be freely mobilized according to prevailing needs. Culture is just one big heap, a garbage dump; riffraff and poor Mona Lisa are there alongside stupid commercials, vulgar and cheap comics, and pop tunes. It is up to the author to hammer out and patch together his own construction—without even having to hide his contempt for the true nature of the material available to him.

Nor is it by chance that Godard so readily turns to wordplays in his agitprop or leafletlike films. Again, the aim is to emphasize the ambivalence of verbalization. Simplicity and simplemindedness are dangerously close here. Flirting with verbal forms and meanings reveals the fragility of words and underlines the presence of the author. But the conventions of film language are ultimately violated in order to throw into sharper relief the distance between the work and its creator, and the moral-political gesture of his observer status. Who is to tell what dominates this behavior, narcissism or asceticism, pride or humility? Or rather, how transparently these blend in with the rectitude of the teacher who wants to teach and educate at all costs!

FILM AS CATALYST, INTERROGATOR, AND JUDGE

Thanks to the camera's ubiquitous curiosity, political education has acquired new possibilities during the last few decades. The temptation to be present as a witness, to have the unquestionable credit of a participant, has offered the film numerous new functions. Haskell Wexler's *Medium Cool* gave an exact picture of our modern society, in which every event may also be its own public double. An event captured on celluloid and simultaneously transmitted spreads in the body of society with a fermenting and provocative effect. Life is no longer locked up or echoless; everything is turned into *news* as it is channeled into the worldwide network of information by the media, distributing and returning everything to the news consumer. This new development was completed, of course, with the technological, sociopsychological revolution of television, but it is true for the cinema as well. The camera's penetration into every nook and cranny, its shameless presence, has become an indubitable social fact: there is no escape from its consequences.

Besides depicting the masses in anonymous terms, film-makers have also been tempted by a more personal interference. Why should only public places be approached? Why could not the individual be asked and interviewed in his own home, in his circle of family and friends, about his relation to his work, his feelings, and his total, uncertain existence? Why could not the ordinary man on the street be questioned, accompanied on his walks, asked whether he is happy or not? Indeed, why not? He could be observed; his gestures, confusion, or exhibitionism, his bitterness or awkwardness in the face of provocation could all be recorded. But once, even if for a brief moment, the victim answers the challenge and gives himself over to the camera's insensitive questions, something happens to him also. He has entered into a relationship with the camera, accepted it as a partner, thereby giving new forms and adding new nuances to his behavior and to the notions of his own role playing. The inquiring camera has then ceased to be innocent. It has become a disturbing, aggressive actor on the stage of everyday life.

This was the jumping-off point for those films of the early 1960s that insisted on interrogating reality. The crossing of borders between art and life or between medium and its object acquired deeper and deeper meaning. A merger of observer and observed was taking place, making clear that the process went far beyond the objective-recording function of the camera. It was not enough that the artistically ordered life was replaced by actual life processed before the camera, but witness became participant and active player—not a receiver but rather a provoker of events. The sensational effects of Jean Rouch's films are due to this attitude. When the heroes of *Moi, un noir* or *La Pyramide humaine* came into contact with Rouch they did not only reveal themselves to the camera; they also realized the often painful truth that they were living different lives, undergoing different experiences from those they normally would have had. The film upset and changed their thoughts, affected their actions and ways of forming relationships; it created and solved conflicts. In a word, the film became something of a demon for them.

Realizing these possibilities had incalculable consequences. Areas of application no one had dreamed of before opened up, for the film had indeed turned into the medium of confrontation, a means of destroying all attempts at beautification or self-deception. It had become a precision instrument to measure the semantics of our gestures and of our self-awareness.

In some respects it has become even more than that. By forcing us to look at our real acts and utterances, it has helped along the processes of rationalization and consciousness raising; it has made us more sensitive to our motivations, thereby opening possibilities for the rearrangement of the ego. *Moi, un noir* is only one of the many spectacular examples of how the hero arrives at a new state of self-awareness by having seen himself on the screen, commenting on his own behavior. The completed film is not only the imprint of a changing character but also an instigator of that change—not to mention the fact that it has also faithfully recorded the entire process. It was also during the course of shooting the film that the small community of *La Pyramide humaine* became aware of its prejudices and complicated ways of discrimination against blacks—all of which led to both isolation and overcompensation at the same time. They were shocked to realize how these attitudes still lay at the bottom of their gestures, while on the surface of their consciousness they believed they had overcome them long ago.

A notable Hungarian undertaking, Judit Elek's *Isten mezején (Simple Story)* seems to have realized one of Moholy-Nagy's ideas of over fifty years ago: to test the camera's ability not in a relatively limited period of time—during the filming—but, on the contrary, in a series of life situations, with the patience of many years—to follow the imperceptible changes of a number of human destinies. In this most simple story we can observe the process of maturation from adolescent partner-selection through marriage and childbirth, noting the work of time on faces and in gestures and movements. The thoroughgoing attention of the camera, which leaves out not the smallest details, has naturally affected the lives of the heroes. They are used to the camera as a permanent witness and psychoanalyst of their daily lives. The girls have accepted that their every step is taken before a certain public. This means, of course, that their every action is controlled not only by their own spontaneous judgment but also by being exposed to a more objective, outside observer. Because of their awareness of this, it stands to reason that they have reacted differently to a number of things—perhaps made different decisions than they would have done without the camera—proving how much the observing mechanism affects the observed object. The suicide attempt and the dramatic divorce, for example, are morally rather questionable developments. Who can tell how things might have turned out, without the camera, for the chosen "victims"? The camera's behavior ranges from aggressive intrusion to a gentle presence, but whatever the camera does, it causes new patterns of behavior among its subjects: to live for and with the camera means the acceptance of a public existence beyond the personal, and the possibility of the interiorization of the external world.

There are more reserved ways in which the camera may be present without in the least diminishing its powers of revelation. I am thinking of those process-illuminating films in which the phenomenon to be observed has some inherent and condensed absurdity. This is so in Forman's first films, whose grotesque or derisive tone is due not to stylistic means but to the situations themselves, and to the author's ability (always used good-naturedly) to lay open the rich storehouse of human folly. The fervent zeal of these little people is grotesque because we feel, simultaneously, its dead seriousness and its exaggerated proportions. An orchestra of pensioners is not something laughable in itself. But it cannot be denied that Forman's viewpoint is not exactly one of identification; he is capable of looking at the fallibility and exaggerated actions of these people from the outside as well. And this double view, its two sides dissolving into and reflecting each other, strikes sparks of irony and gentle cruelty.

Andy Warhol and Paul Morrissey's famous films seem, at first sight, to be rather removed from these methods, yet there are a number of similarities worth mentioning. In their films, as in those mentioned above, the clinging to naturalistic facts is arrogantly persistent. The camera will show only what, and only as much of it as, the world is willing to show it. But *that* it will show without gaps or interruptions, and with no consideration for anything whatever. So one can live, loaf around, display lazy appetite and short-lived desire: to the camera it is all the same. Everywhere behind the symbolic titles of *Flesh, Trash,* and *Heat* there pulsates the fatigue of the flesh, a collapse and disintegration remindful of garbage heaps, and an energy-consuming heat. Or perhaps it is all like a slowly declining graph: the depressing sight of entropy flags and grows faint. The style seems to be evaporating. The unattractive moments of vegetation take a comic turn, and irony is created by a finite transparency, as if in the wake of a deep-raking and indifferent X-ray beam.

IN PRAISE OF STORYTELLING

Here is an almost unique example: irony is brought about by charming storytelling and a gentle-cheerful attentiveness. Alain Tanner's *Jonah, Who Will Be Twenty-Five in the Year 2000* surrounds us with a self-doubting humor and the warmth of an always graceful presentation. The lives of four couples, eight strange and crazy young people, clinging and bound together by the whims of chance, unfold before us. Eight marginal survivors try, after 1968 (and they are clearly marked by that memorable year), to find their place in the current historical amnesia.

Tanner's vision leads to a peculiar technique. After so many modernisms, he daringly returns to the most traditional method of telling a story. His fallible and lovable heroes, as if by magic command, appear out of nowhere. There is something basically biological, simple, and warm in their existence. This is what allows for so many surprising and comic turns in their various encounters. They are only a bit more eccentric, just a little more persistent in sticking to their ideas, than others, but this makes the loose flow of the action colorful and ironically effervescent. This is surely a tale in yet another sense: the free surging of events is the realization of a dream, of a bittersweet utopia, without denying for a moment that the heroes' daydreaming about time and history is but the luxury of their temporary freedom. They are looking for the best combination of freedom and compromise with the world, in their half-absurd, half-clownish roles, in an age ripe for neither revolution nor action. The story's rhythm is set by alternating starts and retreats; trial and failure belong together here like light and shadow, but without the story's falling into melodramatic traps.

Fantasies and flights of the imagination fit into the story as smoothly as they follow each other in our consciousness. An image-fragment signals the direction of desires—getting into bed with two girls, eccentric lovemaking—but only for a flash, like the tempting reality of a fleeting thought. These fantasies provide the same ironic relativization as the insertion of historical documents, opening time's framework for playful excursions into the past and the future.

In his first history lesson, Marc delivers a long discourse on time. Using the trivial example of sausages, he wants to illustrate cyclical rhythm, the organic life of nature and society. But time never repeats itself. There is progress among the cycles, and the film, with its own cyclical progression, follows this double movement. Inner divisions and articulations, recurring events, but never the same movements, roll the action forward. The film's slow pace is patterned after the patient gentleness of time. It can demonstrate the unity of radical change as well as its quiet progress, since every natural birth—including a social one—is tied to a given time of ripening and maturation.

Tanner's contemplative tale is about time as history, and also about time as the framework of our activities. It is about the experience of articulating time, the idea that time could be articulated if only we knew its dynamics, possessed the tools with which to regulate it, and learned to endear ourselves to it. The story's arch is constructed out of the fine flow of the plot, a penetrating banality, and a loving treatment of organic, well-rounded forms. The use of structural elements in the film is "democratic": everything seems to be on an equal level of importance, making the film a most beautiful example of metonymic writing, for each contact creates inner rhymes, harmonies, and rich overtones, which just suffice to bring ideas and thoughts to life.

· 5 ·

The Affinities of Film:
Mythologies of Consciousness

THE DEEP-SEA WORLD OF CONSCIOUSNESS

In the preceding chapters we have examined how customs and gestures of everyday life become ceremonial on the screen; how they acquire mythical dimensions by being presented and distributed in the medium of film. Particularly in big-city life have we found those centers and intersections that may be in need of the interpretive support of myths; it is here that the film, with its comprehensive penetrating ability, has performed a unique service during its short history. When we attempted to find the new myths in the structures of banality, we defined not only the sociopsychological role but also the nature of the film medium. For it is in the essence of myth that we accept its truths as self-evident, and that it presents itself as an axiomatic system without revealing the bias of its well-articulated value judgments. If anywhere, it is in the language of the film that this continually evaluating arrangement of things and events may remain hidden. One of the secrets of film's "magical exactness" (Moholy-Nagy) is the captivating authenticity stemming from its unusual proximity to real life.

Lionel Rogosin's *On the Bowery* or Chris Marker's *Le Joli mai* each presented a slice of life, an average dull existence, by simultaneously showing us the process of sample-taking. They drove home their truths that these fragments were by no means unique; on the contrary, their strength lay in the fact that they could be found everywhere and frequently. Thus we could conclude that these films disseminated lifestyle patterns and society's reactions to them; their function was, willy-nilly, one of standardizing, for they presented examples of already realized solutions—be they horrendous or worthy of following.

What happens when the mythicizing mind is confronted not with simple customs and habits of life but with more complex forms of consciousness, even with the consciousness of myth, for example? The uninhibitedness of today's myths has overcome this obstacle too: the will to mythicize may "gobble up" the myths themselves.

I believe that for a long time we have judged the true affinities of the film rather one-sidedly. Of course we have done this with some justification, for, some outstanding but isolated instances aside, there have been no experiments to show that the film has successfully laid siege to spheres beyond physical reality. Kracauer's soberly limiting film-geography—in its own way not at all free of mythicization— seemed correct when, graciously relinquishing the universe, it at- tempted to mark out film's sovereign territory in the narrower realm of everyday physical existence. In the last two decades or so, however, we have witnessed a real landslide. The areas of presentation have expanded, and at last the film began to spread "inward." Exploration of depth, of the different layers of consciousness, got under way as the camera tried to throw light on the mechanisms of *dreams, imagination, memory,* and *thinking*. But the moment these contents made their appearance, they were immediately exposed to "harmful radiation." Revealed inner truths proved to be no different than any other kind of material with regard to the destructive or, more precisely, constructive- destructive influence of the film. Cinema not only reproduced but also further interpreted the facts and laws of our conscience. It has at- tempted with its own weapons to take possession of the "phantoms" of the mind.

THE DREAM MODE

The similarity between dreams and the film has been noted from the very beginning. Sometimes in more poetic tones, sometimes in less, but both film-makers and theoreticians have addressed themselves to this parallel. We recall certain finger exercises of the 1920s, the poetic experiments of Jean Epstein, Germaine Dulac, and René Clair, in which bizarre or mysterious dreamlike experiences were created by unexpected sequences of images, by free play given to time and space, and, mostly, by magically superimposed players and events. The con- centrated power of crowding images, the strange logic of spectacles that evoked associations and could be explained only emotionally, did remind the spectator of the capricious ways of the dream.

The film does not copy dreams, as Susanne Langer so astutely ob- served. If the film is similar to dreams it is because of its mode of presen- tation: "it creates a virtual present, an order of direct apparition. That is the mode of dream." Most characteristic of this method, according to Langer, is that the dreamer is always at the center. Objects, places, and living figures may continually undergo changes around him, but the dreamer remains at the center, dictating his own relation to everything else, and without necessarily having to make an actual appearance. Thus, he gives a unity to the unfolding images and a meaningful form to the spectacle. "The 'dreamed reality' on the screen can move forward and backward because it is really an eternal and ubiquitous, a virtual present. The action of drama goes inexorably forward because it creates a future, a Destiny, the dream mode is an endless Now."[1]

But what does this infinite present mean? What is this magical Now?

Freud pointed out the essence of dream work: condensation and displacement. With this he may have alluded to dream's affinity to all artistic activity, for his entire psychoanalytic method may, in some respect, be considered the working out of the science of tropes: metaphors and their variations. Freud proved that consciousness can operate without logic but not without some guiding dream-image, which also controls the realm that gives birth to logic. The subconscious does not know "because," or "but," etc.—those peculiar conjunctions of syntactic logic—yet the order of relationships is expressed very clearly. Similarities and oppositions appear as images in the dream unifying the various elements.

The easy ways of mutual reflection and projection, the surprising yet natural combination of events, the expansive flow of continuity in which component elements are not always distinguishable, the fairy tale–like omnipresence—perhaps these are the principle factors that create the infinite present referred to above. For in both the dream and the film, time-space mobility seems unhindered—coexistence and mutual interprojection of things demolish traditional time frames. And perhaps at this point film and dream make contact with wish fulfillment, play, and the freedom of the child's imagination. As Rilke so graphically put it: "Not any self-control, or self-limitation . . . , not caution, but a continuous squandering of all perishable values. This way has something naïve and instinctive about it . . . joyous confidence, resembles that period of the unconscious—the period of childhood."

The creative imagination in its most general sense—therefore including myths, the arts, and child's play—resembles dreams in that it is the principal regulator of the tension operating between our conscious and unconscious. And turning the unconscious into conscious means, in both cases, a progression from the general toward the concrete, making demonstrable and visible something impalpable and abstract. Condensation and displacement serve just this purpose. The picturelike representation makes manifest the suppressed, restrained, and therefore unnamable content. Overcoming the unconscious, whether in dreams, play, or in mythical or artistic representation, also means turning the shapeless into sensory experience. What Carlyle called a "thirst for concreteness" is also the "logic of the detour." Making conscious is not simply a process of rationalization, but a seeking out and finding of the hidden truth by means of the senses, aided by sensual and emotional awareness. "The crooked road, the road on which the foot feels the stones, the road which turns back on itself—this is the road of art" (Shklovsky). Even more precisely: "A dance is a walk which is felt; even more accurately: it is a walk which is constructed to be felt."[2]

This kind of "dance," it seems, prevails in mythmaking. It finds joy in movement, delight in controlled action, and it provides us with experiences of wish fulfillment or avoidance of harm. And, again like dream work, it combines elements in order to make real the desirable. The dynamic-visual basic principle of the film follows the dynamic-visual nature of consciousness and carries it from the private into the public realm.

All our dreams, nightmares, and all the "monsters" of hypotheses, abstraction, and metaphysical hunger are called myths by Valéry, for these are all creations of the imagination. Our conscious is made of small dreams out of which thought creates strange and logical formations, but, Valéry maintains, they are all phantoms, creatures of the mind. But precisely in this creativity lies the freedom of the spirit. "We only love what we created." According to this idea, mythicizing is a way of appropriating and interiorizing the world. We make things our own in order to give them life. The concreteness, mobility, and lively images meet the eidetic vividness of the dream mode.

EXPROPRIATION

Consciousness is locked in a dual combat with the phantoms of the "inside" and the "outside," and the film, too, has developed two kinds of strategies. Mythicizing *everyday life*, as we saw in the previous chapter, has primarily offered the film an overabundance of facts and events. The mapping out of *everyday consciousness* came later, and it is not surprising that it was done with the same mythicizing technique.

Here, once again, we must make a short detour in order to clarify our current interpretation of myths. I have mentioned that Roland Barthes's definition seemed most appropriate, according to which myth is defined not by its object, material, or ensemble of ideas, but by its mode of presentation. Not the content but the form of its messages is of primary importance. In other words, myth is defined by the way it makes use of certain messages, social or otherwise. Myth uses material already processed—beliefs, views, concepts already formed—which it then retransmits in its own language. It reflects that peculiar process whereby some fragment of reality, because of historical change, addresses us, becomes "speech." "For myth is that language which was called to life by history," says Barthes.

Thus, myth is a huge and powerful transformer; its interference is far more aggressive than to be satisfied with certain neutral or subservient translating activities: it performs high-voltage amplifying and reductive operations. Its intended purpose is to create a new system of values, to transfer the existing status quo to a *different* level.

Barthes unceremoniously accuses mythical language of theft and expropriation, for it is always adorned with strange feathers. It can build only on something already made. But this "secondariness" does not prevent the myth from developing a very complicated, multilayered system of signs, accommodating itself to the demands of given historical moments, and reacting to the new challenges and psychological needs of the social climate.

The reason for modern myth's pervasiveness and aggressive presence lies precisely in the fact that natural, interpersonal relationships have been replaced by external, institutionalized forms of communication, and these mediators—our modern myths—could not remain innocent. They carry purposes, convey manipulative action between input and output; they are responsible for essential modifications; their special interpretation and expedient reporting serve well-defined ideals.

Should we then, along with Barthes, consider every manifestation of modern myth as fallacy, simplification, and "consoling lies"? Such a verdict might prove to be too harsh.

What is original in Barthes's premise is that he labels as myth everything that falls into the category of interpretation—only action speaks to us unaided. Consequently, not only traditional forms can serve his purposes, but photography, advertising, the press, and the film are equally appropriate stuff of mythical speech, no matter how differently they may affect the public.

It is in this sense that we had to examine the mythicizing role of the film medium, in order to show that the seemingly most objective system of codes is not an uninvolved mediator. Its information and accurate facts are all reflections of the collective mind; that is to say, they are documents of a given period. What is new in the ability of today's film is that it disseminates not only the behavioral patterns of our lives but also our inner workings and motivations.

Barthes has already called attention to the analogy of myths and consciousness. He points out, with Freud, the similarities between latent and manifest content and mythical consciousness in relation to its object. Just as latent content appears somewhat deformed when we encounter it—in dreams or in states of "lapse"—with myths it is form that notifies us of those manipulations with which a given meaning has been processed or transformed. But there is never a perfect correspondence between signifier and signified. Mental "lapse," for example, is always more modest than the content it reveals. Mythical form also simplifies, reducing the range of original meanings. But this is how otherwise hard-to-reach contents are made available for everyday use. In less friendly terms: with a gesture to ward off complications, myth vulgarizes and prepares for consumption cramped and tensely charged reflexes.

This is also what gives meaning to film mythology's omnivorous gluttony. It processes, homogenizes, digests, and popularizes experiences to which the public would otherwise have no access. We may thank the cinema that some signs of the times or fashionable diseases of our century—like alienation, big-city loneliness, or the elaborate functions of dreams—have become common knowledge and spiritual "goods" for the widest possible consumer public.

This statement may sound somewhat disparaging. But while I believe it is justified to a considerable measure, we must go further and distinguish, as precisely as possible, between the two major trends, as traditionally delineated by theoreticians, in the short history of the film. They are, in capsulized form, the Lumière trend, to which belong the film's objectivist, documentarist, true-to-life aspirations, and the second, the feature-fiction trend, which approaches its material with the more daring, stylizing means of other arts. We must state clearly that in terms of lasting values these two trends are not equal. The latter, "Grand Art," and this is an historical fact, has thus far produced far more fragmentary and questionable values than it cares to admit. It is full of "suspect" results and rather doubtful successes, which it has achieved through the above-mentioned process of popularization.

The mythicizing function, however, holds true for both trends, even if the consequences differ in each; cheap or not so cheap pattern-creation —it is all the same thing.

I would further state that qualitative changes in the film are noteworthy precisely in these terms, and that film's emancipation in the last two decades is especially important in light of these changes. Beyond the fierce and often clumsy competition between the trends, we have also witnessed a whole series of new discoveries. A new era of developing tropes, cinematic and mythic, has begun.

·6·

The Language of Indirectness:
Metaphoric Writing

BARBARIC METAPHOR

If metonymic writing, as we have called it, is direct and clings to reality, its opposite and complementary partner is metaphoric writing, which leads us into the world of the indirect style. The latter mode is not characterized by horizontal, syntagmatic construction, but by the very denial of it; it makes use of vertical, paradigmatic, and daring associations. The gesture of exploding, getting in and out of the natural dimensions of reality, is like the adventures of Icarus; it is a naked challenge. This method facilitates self-reflection and ensures the prominence of the author by emphasizing the deviations more than the recurring movements, by changes and exchanges of places and objects that convey the enjoyment of freedom and the exuberance of playing. In the world of tropes, metaphor is no longer the poor servant, but the flirtatious whore, the very embodiment of an idea. It is neither allusion, reminder, nor parallel and analogy, but an aggressive conquest, an elbowing, sensual reality, the transvaluation of customary objects and meanings. The metaphor is the most immodestly personal form of all poetic means. It is arbitrary, a provocation applied without tenderness, as in *8½*—the spa scene, with its bizarre procession of withered bodies, or the magical atmosphere of the circus—or in Makavejev's *WR*—the Russian ice skater's world of sweet-rotten eroticism—or in Wajda's historical garbage dump. The striking and impolite suggestiveness of the images lends a barbaric character to these metaphors.

The paradox of the method is that it brings together never-known associations, unexpected relationships, and it does so with an unquestionable rectitude. And although this metaphor lacks antecedents, it is immediately understandable. This organic, experiencelike presentation makes it appropriate for mythical expression. Dovzhenko alluded to the desirability of the female body with the super close-up of an apple covered with dew drops. The metaphor was correct and appropriate, only its originality has faded a little with time. But when a real swarming ant-heap covers the entire screen in *Un Chien andalou*, or when in Ferreri's *La Grande bouffe* the inexhaustible gastronomical micracles make one literally drool to the point of nausea, or when in Bergman's *Silence* we see sweating, biting, clawing, lovemaking females and males, we are looking not at obscenity-as-lack-of-taste or at an ignoble straining for effect, but at a barbaric metaphor, which affects us with its objectivity and suggests, makes visible and graphic, its content with a materiality suited to the nature of film.

Pasolini speaks of the ancient, irregular, and barbaric symbolism of images, which is rooted in the peculiar poetry of dreams, visions, and memories, gaining its prototypes from these same sources. We are, indeed, talking about those fortunate exaggerations and intensifications that hit upon the illuminatingly characteristic with intuition and imagination.

By its nature, the image is metaphoric.

Of course, the film's naturalistic tendencies have never been questioned—only its possible value and usefulness. In one of his early writings Lukács, for instance, called the world of the movies "life without presence, life without reasons, motifs, background and perspective, without weight or qualities. The film is a life without essence and value, law and order; it is made of pure surface."[1] Hence its exclusive empiricism, its character that excludes all metaphysics.

But is it possible that direct experience, the standard of empiric existence, would exclude the possibility of our realizing a more abstract spiritual level? Is this not precisely the great lesson of the film: to spark poetry out of mere existence, and to shape mental states into images? Naturally, this sphere touches off different images; impressions and associations acquired here set different parts of our consciousness into motion. Still, we have every reason to believe that through this channel too we can reach an emotional-conceptual synthesis that may be not limited but rather strengthened by retaining the marks of the full-blooded sensuousness and rough lifelikeness of the original stimuli.

It would be hard to find a more painfully detailed description of agony than Bergman's *Cries and Whispers*. With almost unbearable persistence, he shows us the gasping, helplessly writhing body. But while we are looking at the chapped, bloodless lips and hear the grating cries of pain, what we see is not simply the suffering of a woman; it is something much more general; it is death's prose, its obscene destruction.

Or is it by chance that Chytilová, in *Daisies*, shows us the ecstasy of human parasitism, and a playful mood turning into rampage through the image of a grande bouffe? The nature of this fiendish gluttony is that it has a strict physical reality. The headlong wild ride is dictated by the body, its hunger, fatigue, vitality, and selfishness. To circumscribe such a sensually charged state and to give it a highly dramatic impetus appears to be a talent that might lead to the oft-demanded metaphysical capability of the film.

BLASPHEMY

Buñuel's films were among the first to fulfill cinema's metaphor-making function. Even his early, scandal-provoking works achieved their effects by destroying and creating myths, giving a metaphoric extension to our convention-protected customs. The target of his vehement attacks was, in fact, the most secret, yet most common, world of the myths of bourgeois existence. With the liberation of the subconscious, thanks to Freud, suddenly the deepest layers of things suppressed and unsaid came to the surface. Buñuel claimed a foothold here, and, standing among the crumbling sets and suspicious properties of this stage of lies, he proceeded to warn us about the fatal rules of playacting.

His films, understandably, are built on brutal confrontations: reality and illusion, positive and negative aspects, right side and wrong side of the same phenomenon are put on a collision course in order to get closer to some truth. Basic to this method is the frequent use of compact symbols. Some of these have become classic, overquoted examples of film history, such as the symbol created by the sign-ensemble of piano, slaughtered animals, and priests in *Un Chien Andalou*, or the surrealistic visions of *L'Age d'Or*: the scorpion motif and the derisively obscene dream-fulfillment with the cow in the four-poster bed. All these, however, appear to be but savage preludes to the later, more comprehensive undertakings. *Viridiana, The Exterminating Angel*, and *The Milky Way* go much further in the process of condensation, and the entire fabric of these films is interwoven with metaphors. It would be hard to find a better illustration than Buñuel's films for our basic premise, namely that reshaping or stressing beyond limits already-existing primary myths may be an extremely rich potential for cinematic representation.

The underlying thought of *Viridiana* is blasphemy, an acerbic mocking of sacrifice; *The Exterminating Angel* is a transposition of well-known legendary motifs dealing with divine punishment of degenerate sinners; while *The Milky Way* is the most sacrilegious satire of our hypocritic pilgrimages and holy attitudinizing.

There is no need to examine here all the very familiar Buñuelian symbols—the repeated allusions to the Last Supper, the truly biblical significance of the lamb and the bear, or the whole family of Freudian dream symbols. Rather, we are interested in the process—how Buñuel applies and builds into his own conceptions these borrowed elements.

Buñuel's almost unique deed is that he erects no walls of any kind between illusion and reality, between direct allusion and other comparisons. There is no difference in matter or method between the two regions of life: both have the same inevitability. This may be seen, perhaps most clearly, in *The Exterminating Angel*. The tense mysteriousness of the film ultimately stems from this imperceptibility: curse or affliction are intangible. We are made to perceive the imperceptible consequences of an invisible secret. We are to read the nature and extent of changes from tiny signs, the irregularity and distortions of sharply defined, exact gestures. Concealment and revelation powerfully emphasize, like a curtain, the reality that may only be guessed at: these people have been condemned to imprisonment, and the more they want to ignore their sentence the more complete their captivity becomes.

There is, however, a duality to the nature of this prison. Beside its social significance—the drama of the bourgeois order's historical failure —there takes shape another, more metaphysical truth: the emptiness of our existence, which is ruled, having been deprived of divine providence, by man's bewilderment. Man is not only lost himself; he cannot find the key to the way out of his prison either. The situation is further complicated by a most mysterious and unexpected solution to the problem, for it is not a conscious decision but a vague and hesitant attempt that leads to a fresh start. And if man does find his way back to the haven of some starting point, can that be considered real safety or merely a brief respite before a deeper and more unavoidable fiasco: the threat of annihilation?

While reenacting the sinful and destructive adventure, a carefree golden age returns once more to Providence Street. As if in some collective psychoanalysis, people find their lost certainty and the tranquility of the good old days. Behind them are all the awful experiences: violation of sexual taboos, greed, murderous selfishness, illness, and death. In this journey of perdition, biblical rites are repeated, from drawing water and offering a lamb to the liberating act of human sacrifice. But it is all in vain, for it is precisely the future that is lacking in these people's fate. And therefore death is meaningless, since no salvation can come in its wake.

To say that concrete events and their mythical extensions are equally, "palpably" suggestive in Buñuel's work is also to say that in fact the physical existence of activities contains their metaphysical existence as well. Thus it happens that in a suffocatingly real environment dripping with blood and sweat, the "fantastic" or the impossible can enjoy an equally material life. The severed hand crossing the room is, as in our most frightening dreams, a sensory image, no less than the spilled blood of lambs on the carpet or the smashed window, which, in the most literary sense, breaks in order let some fresh, nourishing air into the prison.

Buñuel's method can be interpreted as more than a "homogenizing" process, for the swift integration into the text of archaic and archetypal symbols goes beyond simple "profaning" and the sacrilegious use of symbols. It may also be viewed as a sudden suspension of everyday things and a "tearing loose" toward some undesirable new dimension.

In this sense, the method has a disintegrating function. The aggressive interruption of smooth continuity is a means of establishing interpretive distance, irony. Thus, metaphoric writing will become the basic method of alternating viewpoints and complex structuring. Paradoxically, the stronger the quoted symbol, the stronger the experience of interference. In the parlance of Lévi-Strauss, processing, the "well-cooked" state, and creative transformation are ensured here by the exceptionally articulated and aggressive sensory appeal of the "raw materials."

THE BEAUTY OF SIN AND THE SIN OF BEAUTY

It is well known that Bergman's most frequent theme is man robbed of his transcendence. But while Buñuel, in a mocking mood, yanks these stumbling travelers of hell's circles into blasphemy, Bergman closely identifies with them and descends into the domain of pain and loneliness. Most of his films portray some variation of a bleak existence, where feelings of emptiness and desperation allow "anything to happen." Unalterable experience has created the Bergman aura as well as the few characteristic and constantly recurring elements of the Bergman vision —the sea and the island, for example, seen in a white night with sharply contoured shadows and coldly brilliant waves. There is an impenetrability emanating from all these elements, while the major tone of his landscapes is silence. And the landscape is a mutely echoing labyrinth, the locale of exile and failure, appointed place of assignations, where the protagonists do not meet but chase each other hopelessly "under the cool and empty sky."

This cheerless and ominous world is *beautiful*, for its mysteriousness and inaccessibility hide not only secrets but also the law, the imperturbable truth that is above and independent of man's dwarflike stature. The sea, the wind, the rocks, and the storm all speak of a strict providence, which strikes with alternately more gentle and more punitive blows. These distant islands with their pebbly shores, narrow jetties whose proportions are as nothing compared to the great oceans, are images of a counterworld. Bergman empties this counterworld on purpose, clearing it of everything that might be too concrete or definite, that would tie it to a specific time, space, or civilization. Only the very essential objects and means of existence may appear: a rustically simple stone house, a boat, and windows, disturbingly inviting, that look into the distance, onto the water and the passing clouds covering the sun, and onto the wind fingering the water's surface. Occasionally a distant foghorn splits the quiet dawn, like a message from afar, like a blurred memory of a never realized possibility, like a useless message that evokes no echo. . . .

The more artistic this environment, the more merciless the verdict it pronounces. Its grandeur and majesty are not for man: it offers him neither refuge nor balm. The world is cool and orderly—it has fascinating secrets—while man is all frailty, blemished realization, a prisoner of inexact, distorted, and diseased instincts.

At times Bergman approaches the promising transcendence of art also, but he has very little good to say about it. Art is the work of vampires, it is a murderous adventure, nothing inhuman is alien to it. In *Rite, The Seventh Seal, Sawdust and Tinsel,* and most clearly in *Persona,* Bergman is looking for the secret of this transcendence, this damned and doomed game, the ambiguity of parasitic existence, which is capable of creating only at the cost of others' destruction.

Indeed, art is the vision of beauty, but it is also of dubious value. We may suspect, on the one hand, its origin, that shameless immorality and not so venial clowning, which may be the only basis for creativity —see *Rite* and *Persona*—and, on the other hand, we may question its effectiveness as well as its ephemeral nature. Art has no durability with which to justify itself. The moment we gulp down the wine of beauty and empty the cup that held the secret, as illustrated in *Rite,* we instantly annihilate the shadowy silhouette. The life and death of beauty are one and the same thing. It is born only to be absorbed by and to die in others.

But the question can immediately be turned around: Is it only art that thrives on blood? What about the recipient of art? Is not the latter a consumer of the artist's blood, suffering, sweat, pain and self-destruction? We have come full circle then: we are all man-eaters—the artist's only sin, perhaps, is that he bluntly reveals his own cannibalism.

Bergman's films are of interest to us, for their subject is always some abstract reflection. Everyday events and human gestures are seen, most of the time, not simply as psychological manifestations,

but rather as metaphoric embodiments of a thought, as tortured medi-
tations or confessions. They are paradigms, possibilities of existence
full of lessons to be learned. The bases of his films are death and
diseased instincts, and the modern myths of faith and creativity. What
is peculiar in the way Bergman puts these on the screen is that he lends
them an even further mythical coloring. He does this primarily by
universalizing the world he presents, however fragmentary it may
appear. His heroes can never be anything less than beings marked by
fate; everything that happens to them is predestined, as if they were
ruled by an invisible power. They may struggle, fall, doubt, and atone
their sins, but all this follows, to the letter, an awesome verdict.

Consider the *danse macabre* on the desolate ridge in *The Seventh Seal.*
Mortality and immortality hold on to each other with disturbing mystery—and a playfulness beyond our comprehension—as we watch the
figures grope for one another's hands. This is a ceremony of leave-
taking, which hopes to befriend death by lifting the latter's dark veil;
it is a pagan festival, a gift bestowed upon the players once the ter-
restrial game is over.

Bergman's heroes are always fallible, prone to sin. They are purposefully so. In their helplessness we see the vision of a world deserted
by God, a "negative imprint," as Bergman calls it. What rules here
is a higher law defined by this lack, and the unfriendly truth of a
divinity that is beyond individual existence and that manifests itself
in the paradox of nonexistence.

For this reason, Bergman's metaphysics is the most "biological"
among all his contemporaries. He polarizes the different spheres of
existence to the extreme. If the sin of everyday existence is the loss
of transcendence, it stands to reason that all its efforts are but the vain
ambition of the flesh. And the empty skies have no answers; they only
cause a longing for warmth and beauty. Desire, insatiable hunger, an
introverted selfishness make up man's only motivating reality.

Bergman also creates the structure of his language out of this polar-
ized tension. Cruel and raw biological existence is placed opposite a
mystery, which is nature the unknowable and eternal. The constants
of his world of images carry this message above all: earthly and
heavenly hell never meet.

REPETITION—CORROSION OF TIME

The third great "B," Bresson, is related to his colleagues only in that
the exclusive subject of his films is the lack of grace. Otherwise he
goes his own way; neither the playfulness and derision of Buñuel
nor the painful empathy of Bergman finds room in Bresson's cool

attitude. He does not evaluate or pity; he is looking for the causes of failure and the seed of salvation in his heroes. Ordinary mortal sin does not shock him at all; on the contrary: heavy punishment, he seems to imply, is all the more deserved for pride and lack of humility. Whoever is guilty of these sins condemns himself; there is no inner peace for man without abnegation and the renunciation of selfishness.

For Bresson the state of grace is the state of freedom, and vice versa. But how to achieve this? The road leading there is not only hard but also difficult to find. This is why most of the time the calvary of his heroes ends in failure: they grope and suffer, pursued by their desires, trying to find a way out. As if afflicted with blindness—not seeing themselves, and even less able to see others—they are doomed to stumbling about and marking time.

Perhaps this is what accounts for the icy, glittering, and gothic asceticism of Bresson's language. For the outside world, with all its features and historical development, is nothing but a false stage set. Bresson is looking for the road leading to the inner world, to ourselves. Only thus can he hope to give spiritual meaning to the spectacle, which, of necessity, is untainted by emotions and dramatic intensification. In all his films he speaks of one thing: man's loss of grace, the adventure of those who must do without the metaphysical world. In Bresson, the metaphor of this echoless effort has found its master poet of human passions.

It may seem strange how readily this apparently so anti-Dostoyevskian artist turns to Dostoyevsky. In certain vital issues, however, the two may not be so far apart. What attracts Bresson primarily to the Russian novelist is the latter's concept of sin—sin as trial, as an organic part of existence, as a constant station of man's unavoidable calvary; he agrees with the interchangeability of sinner and judge before a higher authority. Jeanne d'Arc and the Gambler both fail in their earthly careers, but it is certain that this is not equally valid for both in terms of passing a test of conscience. And in another example, let us consider how much of the same stuff the condemned and the pickpocket are made of! For the world of real purposes is to be sought not in practical life but in the realm of spiritual freedom. And there it makes no difference what kind of activities have annealed the soul, what sort of direct challenge has led to one's purification and self-acceptance. Suffering, then, is not an affliction, but simply an attitude toward fate, part of accepting and acknowledging passion, man's capacity for contrition and humility.

These may be the symbols of religion, but Bresson has nothing to do with traditional symbols. His myth is built, rather, on the denial of tradition. Wrestling with the angel, for example, has been internalized, and Bresson's true locale is *time*. No other director has managed to dress bare and inanimate objects in such sensuous time dimensions. They are carriers of nerve-grinding emptiness of nonpassing time, of a corrosive slowness. The spectacle, the almost infinite time of images, is filled with antispiritual and naked materiality; objects are magically extended by a painstaking focus on physical details. The prison walls (in *A Man Escaped* and in *The Trial of Joan of Arc*), the heavy doors, the stairs, the flagstones leading to the stakes, are all dead, or, if you will, environmental elements; neither anthropomorphic depiction not enlargement is used here to give them added meaning. Bresson's is a different method of mythicizing. *Repetition*, the stubborn reality of reiteration, is his major weapon. Emphasis is achieved by the oppressive regularity of recurrences: to face again and again the dreary and unembellished details. This repetition, of course, is rich in connotations evoking, first of all, the power of rituals. Whether looking at this from the viewpoint of "positive" human will—as in the case of the creative gestures of one preparing his escape with infinite patience—or in its "negative" application, resistance broken by oppression, repetition contains a heavy presence and a merciless order that are beyond the individual. In the unusually vacant world of Bresson, man's seemingly uncertain steps are guided by the monotony of repetition and the maniacal, hypnotic rhythm of recurrences.

Susan Sontag talks about the "physics of the soul" in connection with Bresson. Taken literally, the paradox seems fitting: the unity of spiritual and physical forces is embodied in a peculiar exchange in Bresson's films. The sensuous-concrete image is filled with spiritual significance, and, conversely, the spiritual content—the most abstract imperatives of ethics—acquires an objective-physical reality. Although the invisible can be followed only in the description of a near-empty environment restricted to the spectacle of very few components, the antidramatic analysis is still charged with real tension, for at its bottom a relentless progress is under way. Time is at work, and in the apparent non-happening a thousand tiny events are concentrated.

THE LIBERATION OF TIME

When considering film's sensitivity to time and various temporal structures, we take into account some of the basic peculiarities discovered by cognitive psychology. As we have seen, the road from sensory-motor intelligence to the articulate expression of thought is rather long, but its stations, with appropriate adjustments of course, are not all that difficult to trace in the development and gradually maturing intelligence of the film.

Piaget pointed out that one of the most important of mental activities is the reversibility of operations. Without this ability things could not be traced back to their origins, changes could not be rectified, their values could not be measured. Transition from raw empiricism to mental recognition begins at the point where we are able to traverse events in both directions: to start at beginnings and reach consequences, and vice versa. This movement from parts to whole, from cause to effect, from operating forces to final results, is never straight; it includes "backing up" maneuvers, detours, and interactions of its various factors.

Irreversibility is in the nature of things—the mind's mission is to transpose things into reversible forms.

The liberation of time, which is to say the escape from time's linear, one-directional, and single-purpose flow, is the greatest achievement of cognitive activity; it is the alpha and omega of every kind of thinking and abstraction.

The unavoidable articulation of time was also a principal condition in the development of film-thinking. In cinema's "prehistory" only a very primitive mode of interrupting time was known. Early movies, understandably, delighted in their ability to follow the actual movement of events, the natural passing of time. Only much later did the film reach that contracting-mimetic evocation that already included abstraction by stretching and shrinking real time processes. Then, a method of breaking up the present was born: the flashback technique, which was to serve the purpose of resurrecting the past. This was the first decisive step toward violating time's irreversibility. It was hesitant, often uncertain and awkward, but it did cross the border, paving the way for an operational arrangement and intellectual structuring of things.

In our cognition, the irreversibility of events and their reversibility through mental processes appear to dovetail. This cognitive ability gives us the indispensable dialectic with which to express simultaneously what is permanent and what is ephemeral. In fact, we may express the lasting only by circumscribing the transitory, by cutting up an event in such a way that we go beyond it, break it down into its components —which is to say that we move freely back and forth in time.

Not only time's flow and penetration into space articulates the message; it is also the space-exploring movement that fills out, organizes, and explains duration, the time of the experience. There is no interpretive system made of mobile components that would not include, in some form, the element of time. Without manageable time, without its liberation, without the freedom to arrange and rearrange its units, we cannot speak about any kind of intellectual activity. Interruption, cutting, the arbitrary breaking and resumption of processes were also part of film's early striving for an articulate language. Discontinuity has become the starting point of all structures.

If in heterogeneity we have come to see the film's peculiar system of spatial relationships (i.e., tensions being achieved by the juxtaposition of dissimilarities), we may consider discontinuity as the factor that determines the film's temporal relationships and its organizing principles.

Film's only continuity is a series of discontinuities, the arbitrary desertion of realistic processes, an optional noting of starting and terminal points. Ultimately, it is the free juxtaposition of time-quanta that produces the artificial universe of the film, its self-created space-time continuum.

This achievement, as I have mentioned earlier, is the consequence of certain historical developments. It is true of the film also that to get from direct action to an "interiorized intelligence," a certain road must be traversed in which the use of symbols plays an important role. Piaget, regarding the structures of categorical thinking, emphasizes the not-totally new. All subsequent substructures, including the concept of the subject, time and space, and causality, are already precisely constructed in the "first" phase. But there is a need for a certain decentralization in order to develop a comprehensive mental flexibility. A whole series of symbols appears gradually, facilitating abstract thinking and a system of interiorized activities that ultimately leads to mental operations. And the essence of these operations is nothing but the coordination of reversible activities, their integration into a new and complete system. If this is so, then this station of cognitive development is not one of interpretation (i.e., transposition into language), but of a restructuring—in other words, the establishment of a new, self-explanatory and self-fulfilling system. As we can see, the use of alternating viewpoints and changing positions is vital to this process. The "decentralization" of film language—often referred to as the emancipation of the camera—follows this process in that a completely free articulation and reconstruction of time accompanies the free use of space. Every logic is the logic of *relationships*. Like all other modes of cognition, film's increased refinement may be measured by the complex network of relationships it is capable of creating.

Conceptual logic's most mature phase is based, according to Piaget, on two characteristics: one is the combinatory capacity, i.e., instead of a consecutive series, the possibility of relating any element to any other; the second is "the classification of all classifications, or the arrangement of all arrangements." Conceptual logic means combining all the different groups into one system, in which *inversion, reciprocity, correlation,* and *identity* are all equal possibilities of reversibility. In-unity. The mysteries of the human organism reveal—not at all in mysterious operations—bio-psycho-political secrets, those rippling consequences that, bluntly put, are caused by the lack of freedom. From newsreel fragments to interviews, from nightmarish fiction to quotations of the silent cinema, the field is infinitely wide, heterogenous, and incommensurable. With the greatest of ease, the medium of the film gathers everything these sources have to offer in one great bouquet, and thus thought may burst forth with an increasingly greater didactic openness, as everything rushes and points to the same goal.

The method is even wittier, and so is the truth, in *Sweet Movie*. We are presented with a picture of a gigantic consumer market, aggressive and universal, of an omnivorous hunger that no longer feasts on goods but on human ideas, revolutionary and reactionary ideals, greediness, outraged illusions, and feelings that have been turned into merchandise; beauty and desire are gobbled up with the same unstoppable appetite. Images of a ship bearing a revolutionary emblem, a sugar cemetery, a sex-bomb from an advertisement, and nylon-covered corpses of children follow each other in shocking succession: brutal, obscene tableaux, whose playfulness is "deadly" and whose seriousness is as ironic as it is impossible. "L'humor est la politesse du desespoir," said Breton. It is not so difficult to recognize in the grotesque the "unacceptable" sadness and the bitter strength of "sweetness." Lucidity and outrage, understanding and empathy juxtapose far-removed elements. Distortions, aggressive symbols (Marx's giant face with a prophylactic rubber as a tear, the chocolate bath, the barbarity of therapeutic regression), and the most daring jumps of the imagination keep shocking us, lifting us up, and pushing us under. The individual details begin to wind themselves around one another; their different tones grow more harmonious, their relationship more organic—the medium's mythicizing-homogenizing power transfigures their meaning.

Basil Wright is correct in calling Makavejev the prophet not of doom but of joy. "He takes aim at the masturbatory basis of this age of concentration camps and birdbrains. Where Godard suffers of constipation, Makavejev brings benevolent relief to the intestines. . . ." Makavejev himself strengthens this liberating goal: "I believe there is an existential libido in every film, some sort of erotic energy which is based on visual images, a life energy. . . ."[2] And indeed, this dynamic, this life energy, nourishes and explains the delight of his arrogant jokes, harsh and blasphemous gestures. Ultimately, his is an invitation to a bittersweet dance, the dance of freedom.

In the last scene of Věra Chytilová's *Daisies*, the two little insatiable stomachs gone berserk after an endless eating spree swing their

THE CONSTELLATION OF RELATIONS

McLuhan asserts that "now, . . . in the electronic age, data classification yields to pattern recognition. . . . when data move instantly,
classification is too fragmentary in order to cope with data at electronic
speed. In typical situations of 'information overload,' men resort to the
study of configuration."[3] Thus it is the novelty of the electronic age
that we are led out of the world of succession and combination into
a world of configuration and creative structuring. Is not the film
medium exactly the one that may represent the transition from linear
relations to configuration?

The true paradox is that the film takes us closer to global seeing
by carrying out this fragmentary principle. How is this possible? The
answer is that every comprehensive viewpoint, or any complex process,
when molded into a single model, requires a particular structure of its
own, namely, one in which the component elements and lines of force
are visible. Structure does not hide; rather it shows itself forth, since
the message is conveyed by the planned proportions and defined arrangement of the means used.

Here, there is indeed no validity to gradual development. A live
structure, an organically functioning model, may be constructed only
of small units which themselves are organic entities. In this way,
various parts and details sliced into a cross-section at any moment, will
still show life and will embody the configuration characteristic of the
whole model.

The example of *Casanova* may illustrate this point. Casanova has no
story—only fate. This "destiny" determines, with recurring sameness,
his every moment and any situation he may be involved in. His relationships are always the same sort and follow the same pattern: the
gestures of approach, desire, and disgust are regulated by a single inner
tendency—be it a blessing or a curse. Whenever we catch Casanova,
we are always at the right place at the right time. Is there any sense
then talking about "development" or realistic progress? Is it not more
important to be aware of what is being expressed in each constellation?
Or let us take Buñuel's *That Obscure Object of Desire*. The basis of the
drama is the continual replaying of one fundamental pattern: the trap
of the hero's schizophrenic desire, alternating between attraction and
repulsion. He too, like Casanova, is characterized by a constellation
of frequent and seesawing emotional relations and by those variations
of delicate shades and fine nuances in which we experience the unity of
repetition and change.

In *Teorema*, Pasolini has also found a way to express his theme
in a model-like, kaleidoscopic structure. Unfolding variations and car-

rying them to a conclusion with an almost pedantic determination, as if to prove a hypothesis, seemed to be the most appropriate approach for the film. Analysis and synthesis are realized in the series of configurations, but the essence of the model is that it has but one key, which, when found, will open the door to all the model's secrets. Modifications of the basic situation are all clues to the laws of the overall structure. No wonder that we often feel these films to be too cool and calculatedly designed. Reliance on model-like structures indeed ensures a special place for disciplined consciousness.

In Jancsó's films, relationships are most directly expressed by a geometry of spatial structuring; their complex meanings are revealed by the relative positioning of the players and by variations on an initial pictorial arrangement. In *Silence and Cry*, for example, movements and characters flowing together or veering off and away, then surrounding and circling a center, are the sole means of conveying the message of the situation. Wittgenstein's statement surely holds true here: "Every image is [not only spatial but] also *logical* . . . the image presents possible situations in a logical space" (italics mine).

MENTAL SPACE—MENTAL TIME

What turns physical, geometrical space into "logical space"; what gives it abstract meaning or mythical dimensions? I have mentioned earlier that in Bergman's, occasionally Bresson's, and the first phase of Jancsó's work, the most frequently used method was that of 'emptying out,' a way of avoiding contingency and any definiteness of space. The reality of a prison cell or a landscape is not historically but only sensuouosly concrete. Similarly, most critics noted of Jancsó's *puszta* that its ominous character is expressed by its bleak infinity as it stretches the horizon between openness and confinement. This space is indeed a highly charged field of force controlled by "the geometry of passions," which is to say that it is articulated by a time undermined by human conflicts and experiences: the constantly threatened time of the present.

If space creates abstract and symbolic power by its confining ability, time functions exactly the opposite way: it complements this same effect with its anxiety-ridden openness. In this respect, the otherwise dissimilar Bergman, Bresson, and Jancsó do meet on common ground, for in the work of all three, what keeps us in suspense is the *unknown* as passing time, as an unstoppable progression. The successive moments add to, subtract from, turn inside out, revoke, or fulfill something in the preceding moment's content, each flaunting its deviations and qualitative emphases. However, like other symbol-constructs that have become almost conceptual, time, too, loses its direct concreteness; it becomes timeless or mental time.

"Stopping" time or the enlargement of time is, of course, tied closely to the film's "eternal present-time," or, as Susanne Langer calls it, its "infinite now." In this time experience, the passing of time can demonstrate only a peculiar paradox: the unsurpassable present, which necessarily absorbs the dimensions of the past and the future. Time is simply "marked," bearing stamps of "was" and "will be." The images carry imprints of all the memories of the just-passed moment, but they show a restless openness too, as we seek to know, but cannot, which ones of the abundantly collected elements will continue to live and which ones will die. If the prisoner we see in the opening shots of *The Roundup* suddenly sets out in an open space toward the horizon, we feel that this freedom bodes ill for him. We are looking at this suspicious, undermined movement and wait tensely for something irrevocable, as the prisoner just keeps going toward the geometric center of the frame, where, we are convinced, something must happen. He cannot go farther. Precisely this tight construction and well-planned solution prepare the end, which, in turn, is so unemphatic that only a fraction of a second may be spent on its perception.

What part of the day, or which season, is signified by the lapping waves, the wind, and the seagull's screeching at dawn, in Bergman's *Through a Glass Darkly?* They call to mind the sensuous reality of the time of sleeplessness, of bad conscience, or perhaps the "hour of the wolf," the time of some mysterious, diabolical power. Here too, the more general the barren spectacle, the more eventlessly concrete the event—which is to say the passing of the time—the weightier and more spiritual, therefore timeless and motionless, it all appears.

On occasion, the method of "populating" may complement and carry similar meaning to the emptying-out approach. Wajda, for instance, or the later Jancsó, is looking for ways to fill out and weave through the entire medium with contradictions, to enmesh it in them. Thus the image becomes multilayered, opening wide the borders of time, creating that temporal width that is able to express the common action-space of otherwise independent elements that are nevertheless coincidental in time.

In Wajda's *Landscape after Battle*, the most important event of the last part is the presentation of the Grünewald pantomime. Parallel to this, a whole series of personal dramatic events is accumulating, each demanding its own place in the overall texture. The method used here is not the usual one of counterpoints or dramatic cross-cuttings, but a rather peculiar generalizing intent, which hopes to give an historical perspective by going beyond the particular. This is why the deliberate inclusion of anachronistic elements is so significant: they must allude to this transcendental gesture of the film, must make conscious the demanding participation of the present time within, or despite, the framework of the ongoing war.

OBSCENE PROXIMITY—VERTIGO

Wajda's example points very clearly to the stylistic methods in which there is neither room for nor interest in the usual tableau-dramaturgy of "historical frescoes." The camera's attention is more penetrating, the showing forth more aggressive; the details acquire the reality of the flesh, an obscene sharpness and sensuality stretching the limits toward the universality of the trivial. The arrogantly freckled skin of the girl, the deep impression of Olbrichsky's wire-framed glasses on the bridge of his nose, and the outrageous sweetness of the German girl's blond hair are spectacles much too powerful for us to consider them secondary. They want to make our own impressions uncomfortable and violent, thus, paradoxically, forcing the process of transcendence. Bitterness and the visceral desires of life seem to hurl us into the abstract heights of experience, toward, if you will, its cognitive generality. Experience is no longer stylization but palpable reality, the unavoidable Now.

In Jancsó's work, for example, a similar technique—unexpected emphases of shocking close-ups—has an entirely different meaning. The super close-ups of the protagonists in *Elektra* or the close-up of the pigeons and the bread in *Red Psalm* are all expressions of an intensified abstraction rather than of an immediate reality. We feel these elements to have been lifted so decisively out of concrete events that we register only their symbolic, archetypal value and not their organic ties with the events. But whether we see them as symbols or not, proximity is the means of generalization, its concreteness "deconcretizes," and the tension thus created is always a moving force.

In *The Wedding*, Wajda further refines this aspect of his language. He articulates the super close-ups with the unusual, dynamic approach of jolting and yanking his camera about. He intensifies the frenzy and drunken dizziness of the wedding to the point of physical nausea, of staggering and falling down. Vertigo is the key element of this style; coarseness reaches its low, or high point on this level. And since movement is always rhythm, the pulsating beat in this film also becomes insufferable as it reaches a crescendo of aggressive sensuality.

The aim here is not to give us only a taste, but rather to involve us, hurl us along and carry us to the limit, by making us lose ourselves in the frightening-attractive sensation of stupor.

In this general exaggeration, abundance and moderation meet, both of them serving the process of transcendence, since unrestrained fever and numbness are part of the selfsame truth.

Because of the powerful directorial vision, the film's evocative character floods its smallest molecules, defining, like a "genetic code," the specific order of the various elements. The great symbol-makers, like tyrants, always follow some obsessive formula with maniacal consistency and fanatic "repetitions." Perhaps each one of them could be described by a single key formula. Style is a unique and incomparable configuration.

FLOWING AND FIXATION

Thinking is nothing else, say the psychologists, than some kind of middle road between the storm of thoughts, referred to as a leap of thought, and an *idee fixe*. Thinking's dialectic is marked by fits and starts and various entanglements—yet it is also directed toward the thorough examination of one goal. The duality of thinking is also expressed in the blending of fixation and flowing.

The same contradiction can be seen rather obviously in the film montage. While it is true that the film is uniquely suggestive in evoking the objective reality of things and in clinging directly to nature, it is also true, and to no less a degree, that the film is deviant in its nimble disappearances, and in its predilection for going beyond the concrete moment. The time-space freedom of the camera allows the coupling of anything with absolutely anything else. Even if the camera lingers over the captivating reality of an object or event, it is capable, at the same time and with great ease, of surrounding this reality with a whirlpool of moods, a stream of rushing memories and ideas—all as flowing images.

Stubborn adherence to reality and capricious digressions may alternate in the stream of the montage, just as in the process of thinking. I have pointed out a number of times that this alternation is a matter neither of whim nor of disorder, and further, that it is by no means a less developed or less mature stage of mental activities. Purposeful achievement, even in the most scientific thinking, is realized only through this detour: changes of rhythm regulated by the imagination.

We must not forget, however, that there are, undoubtedly, such gestures, happenings, and movements of life whose essential characteristic is "disorderliness," an almost untraceable fluctuation. If there is a medium, therefore, which chooses for its structural principle this swirling simultaneity, then we may acquire new information through this mediator. Every realistic movement in the history of the film has proved to be very sensitive to the ephemeral and throbbing nature of the flow of everyday events. Through a series of examples I have tried to show how film has demonstrated this dialectic of chance and necessity in an irregular flow of images. In this approach, metaphoric power is created not only by the simple juxtaposition of diverse images, or by the encounter of unusual spectacles, but also by strongly articulated changes of rhythm. In the rather loose flow of some continuity, there appears an "*ostinato*" theme—the obstinate and conspicuous use of an image or a figure of "speech"—and the tension created between the two, the flowing and the fixed, becomes the nucleus of our experience.

THE MECHANISM OF CONSCIOUSNESS

Between the extremes of the fixed idea and the leaps of thought lies the field where cognition takes place. How does this work, what is the operating mechanism, what sort of model is the one that film follows with its dynamic structure?

One of the most famous examples will, unquestionably, always be Resnais's *Last Year at Marienbad*, whose declared aim was to penetrate somehow behind the defense lines of our consciousness, to seek out its various components and their mutually destructive and constructive interactions. Aristotle had already claimed that "the soul never thinks without images," and thus, when Resnais's *Marienbad* or Robbe-Grillet's somewhat less penetrating *L'Immortelle* attempted to grasp the nature of memory, what they were trying to do was in fact to follow the mechanism with which we bring to life images buried in our memory.

What is the secret of the movement of memories, of their being condemned to death or allowed to live; according to what sort of code do we store them; what is the strength of each fragment's life or its effect for further processing? These are the questions to which psychological research and some films, in their own way, have provided a number of diverse answers in the last few decades. Resnais emphasizes the indivisibility of the remembering conscience: the blending of reality and imagination; crossable and rather uncertain borders of time dimensions are the major underpinnings of this work. Makk's *Love* and *Catsplay* reveal the nostalgic, self-defensive mechanism of imagination and memory. The director has succeeded in demonstrating the peculiar presence of a wild and disorderly storehouse of images, and how it has penetrated the present.

In all instances we are dealing with ceaseless motion. The surging images are proofs supporting visual arguments. The order of any series of images usually appears to be arbitrary, most of the time even shockingly whimsical; still, in its jumps, recurrences, and repetitions, a deep, if subjective, logic is at work. The chain of associations, despite all seeming freedom, is ruthlessly determined.

This logic is valid precisely because it does not operate in some abstract space. It is held taut and tense by the most tightly knit emotional motifs, in which the memories of the past play a role only as much as do the painful needs of the present moment. Among the obsessions of the old lady in *Love*, there is an often returning image of great fascination: four old gentlemen, dressed in tails, lift their hats in greeting. This memory fragment is of no great consequence, yet it has a strange significance, since it keeps recurring, while other, similar images, such as the bobbing boat on the lake, although much more personal, do not recur. There is, obviously, a reason for this stubborn insistence, and the repetition suddenly does produce the poetic emanation of these fragments: they become the symbol of a lifestyle forever locked in the past.

These flashes and recurrences of various duration no longer bear any relationship to the old technique of the flashback. Their function is not the illustrative-coloring interruption, but the demonstration of a continuous presence. They are sending us signals from that layer of our consciousness which is the constantly active background as well as the treacherous base of our actions and thoughts.

With this, the direct, rational cause-and-effect explanation of relationships widens considerably: the more that hidden and secondary motifs, detours, and "gratuitous rests" are all accommodated, and sudden emotions and idiosyncrasies are examined, the closer the explanation comes to illuminating the mechanisms of the mind's processes.

In Peter Watkins's *Munch*, this motivating background appears as a number of basic patterns that define the painter's experience: unforgettable, terrifying, and beautiful memories of childhood.

These pedal-points, of course, flash into sight at the most unexpected moments, only at the command of the tensions produced by the present.

Of course, there is nothing miraculous in that a face, a smile, or a situation can evoke something similar in the remote past; rather, the question is: with what technique does the retrospective allusion blend into the forward-moving happening, or, as in music, how rich and refined in its variations is the "development" section? In the case of film this technique is more complex, for tempo, color, movement, and words are equal contributors to the resulting texture. When does contiguity turn into real touching, to the extent that it can set in motion a whole cluster of memories, a "bunch" of events?

In some modern psychological studies we find two kinds of dreams described: "slender" and "clustered." The former works with relatively little visual material; despite its allegorical significance it seems to have no body. The "clustered," kaleidoscopic dreams, however, are downright inflated: interlocking images and scenes hang together in them with restless inconsistency, almost completely burying the core. This duality may be found in cinematic narration as well, and "clustered" dreams, capable of mobilizing an abundance of images, may easily be associated with our current analysis.

In Glauber Rocha's ballad *Antonio das Mortes*, each symbol-pivot is clustered with changing and differently arranged event-groups, where the association of motifs, and not plot logic, dictates the linking of images. The moments of bloody fights and violence are answered by past(?)-imaginary(?)-mythological(?) scenes, conjuring up an unpredictable garland of painful, poignant, and unbearable dramatic moments. At the same time, a peculiar, ritually festive atmosphere, measured slowness, and dignity stylize the play, powerfully reminding us of the spiritual reality of the spectacle. With this "cluster" as a recurring medium, as with a kind of *epiteton ornans*, the characters gain a mythological extension indeed. Their fate outgrows their physical existence: they recall master and oppressor, the rebel, the untouchable, the forever dying and resurrected man, and eternal femininity.

It is worth mentioning here that in his notes on *Das Kapital*, Eisenstein too connects the associative technique with this "clustered" method. This was part of his search for the possibilities of continuity and dramatic development in the structural tension between an evocative starting point and a multidirectional branching off of images.

PREGNANT MOMENT

If, as we have seen, the film favors such stratification and billowing simultaneity, could we not then speak about the "pregnant moment," known from the world of fine arts, which is the dramatic, illusion-creating means of condensing time?

Thus far we have mentioned stretching, broadening, and widening time, implying, of course, that all these operations have served the purpose of concentration and intensification.

The cinematic paradox of the pregnant moment is that concentration is achieved by a peculiar stretching, by the juxtaposition of image-events whose time-space dimensions are not continuous. Small clumps of happenings and action-fragments are lined up in a series, without any particular order of preference or hierarchy and without showing an express cause-and-effect relationship with one another.

Let us begin with the simplest example, the famous murder scene in Hitchcock's *Psycho*. The single movement of the knifing is "broken down" and stretched out into seventy different shots. Obviously this expanded time factor will increase the psychological effect manifoldly; the means of intensification is the technique of retardation, resulting in a more powerful message.

We find a different kind of symbolism in the case of "gratuitous" lingering over certain objects. In Jakubisko's films, for example, abandoned attics, barns or chicken coops, an inn or a country lane irrevocably become metaphors, for they are so charged with the past, crowded with significance: they are loud lamenters of desolation. Or let us remember the little children, naked, wearing only garlands as they walk through the slaughter; they are innocent and degenerate, unafraid, with the confusing ambiguity of angelic and wicked attitudes. The major motif is "love, folly, and death," blending together, providing an abundance of meaning and illuminating symbols. The recurring symbols strengthen one another: pealing little bells, violated, blood-soaked geese in flight, fluttering white feathers, galloping unbridled horses, an abandoned, bat-infested tower, and rooms full of remains of objects standing guard to the past. And then the group portrait comes into view like a look at oneself, like a playful doubling of the entire action. Whatever we do is a spectacle, in the wide sense of the word, and will serve as example and memory.

The closing shots of Claude Goretta's *The Lacemaker* create a moving and poetic aura of a secret ambiguity by an infinitely stretched "holding" of the image. The whole scene is a near–Mona Lisa smile, no more mysterious than its famous predecessor, but this motionless attention evokes the deepest emotions as it conveys pain and the unbridgeable distance between two people. This one look challenges all certainty, turning serenity into doubt: what is really looking at us—foolishness or wisdom, madness or understanding? The real question, of course, concerns the crossable borders and their uncertainty. What is indeed the difference between suffering and illness; how do we judge and distinguish between angelic superiority and complete alienation?

This is the countenance of a simple soul doomed to loneliness, but in this injured look there lurks not only sensitivity but perhaps a bit of irony as well. Beyond demands and selfishness, still this side of total resignation, she is surrounded by a warmth, but this warmth accuses; it is an uncomplaining complaint, a warning. We are confused and somewhat shamed by it, for it is a sad consolation of a broken and doubtful human victory; it is outside of time; it is timeless. Compensation here is only the abstract transcendence of mercy and morality.

Finally, as a last example of serial treatment, let us consider the closing shots of Jancsó's *Agnus Dei*. The only comprehensive metaphor of the film is the *danse macabre;* the successive moments and actions are connected neither logically nor chronologically: their meaning is derived only from this central metaphor. The diabolical violinist is strolling about; in the background a detail of white-clad figures destroy their victim; to the side there is a towering stake already ablaze, and naked boys and girls walk submissively into the fire. The violin plays; the death march is much like a graceful dance; crackling, sizzling logs fill the screen.

A great number of motifs are crowded into this spectacular choreography. The ensemble of social and psychological, magical and historical forces leads to the final accounting. Center stage is claimed now by the killing, now by the bizarre artistry of music and gesture, now by the terrifying lyricism of the death dance, now by the raw natural physical reality. All this is caught up in one continuous action, in the single white-hot "pregnant moment" of multiple significance. The alternating configurations of these elements show us in the end the rich panorama of destruction, its range arched between the most brutal and the spellbinding.

It is true that the ultimate content and meaning of each situation is always the same, but the nuances and direct manifestation are different. Precisely in this variegated sameness can we see the categorical —if you will, conceptual—structure of murder. While the various parts line up on a seemingly arbitrary scale and make no effort at contact, we nevertheless feel that there is one constant factor rising above all the parts. Long takes and the comprehensive continuity of all camera movements underline this inner coherence. In the end the juxtaposed structural elements lead us—although on routes other than logic's induction or deduction—to some synthesis. And since neither a single phenomenon nor a structural element is allowed a distinguished role, this reserved attitude proves rather double-edged: complexity becomes the aggressive representative of openness.

And here we are, so close to our vocabulary of the twenties: film as "the transmutation of ideas into things" or film as "touching the skin of things" (Artaud). The film of ideas is always energy as well, the apotheosis of movement. "Generative film, " the multiplying power of images, "ideo-reality," compulsory ambivalence, and openness are the shocking combination of contradictions: concepts that have lost none of their meaning in the last fifty years. If metaphoric expression also favors this "convulsive beauty," we would do well to recall the same expression's provocative-cathartic ambition. Its dynamic complexity, its content-structural pluralism, may make the film into its own wonderful medium: "Everything you can think of, however vast or inclusive, has in the pluralistic world view a genuinely 'external' environment of some sort or amount," writes William James. "Things are 'with' one another in many ways, but nothing includes everything, or dominates over everything. The word 'and' trails along after every sentence. Something always escapes."

The film, by its nature, I believe, answers this need. Its concreteness and reifying nature, and its provoking, pluralistic structure faithfully reflect and communicate the dialectic of the unity of divergence. Things remain things with a life of their own, and through this never-to-be-caught self and reality, they signal what is beyond. "The pluralistic world is thus more like a federal republic than like an empire or kingdom," James continues. "However much may be collected, however much may report itself as present at any effective center of consciousness or action, something else is self-governed and absent and unreduced to unity."

Film opens up for us this inexhaustible and inaccessible zone, too. It invites us to follow it, but it calls us only for the exploration, promising no arrival. This invitation is perhaps the most convincing proof of film's transcendence.

Notes

CHAPTER 1: *Introduction*

1. *Authors on Film,* ed. Harry M. Geduld (Bloomington: Indiana University Press, 1972), pp. 130–31.
2. Dziga Vertov, *Articles, journaux, projets* (Paris: *Cahiers du Cinéma,* 1972), p. 19.
3. Jurij Lotman, *Semiotics of Cinema* (Ann Arbor: Michigan Slavic Publications, 1976).
4. Jean Baudrillard, *L'Échange symbolique et la mort* (Paris: Gallimard, 1976), p. 112.
5. Ibid., pp. 114, 117.

CHAPTER 2: *Means and Potentials of Film-Thought*

1. In *L'Art du cinema,* ed. Pierre Lherminier (Paris: Seghers, 1950), p. 589.
2. Ferenc Mérei, "Az Utalás" ("Allusion"), in *Szemiotikai Tanulmányok* (Budapest: MTA, 1976).
3. Ibid.
4. Claude Lévi-Strauss, *The Savage Mind* (Chicago: University of Chicago Press, 1966), p. 35.
5. Ibid., p. 36.
6. Ibid.
7. Lev S. Vygotsky, *Thought and Language,* ed. Gertrude Vakar, trans. Eugenia Hanfmann (Cambridge: MIT Press, 1962), pp. 126–27.
8. Ibid., p. 125.
9. *Filmkultura* (Budapest), 1968.
10. In *Film: A Montage of Theories,* ed. Richard D. MacCann (New York: Dutton, 1966), p. 315.
11. In *Movies and Methods,* ed. Bill Nichols (Berkeley: University of California Press, 1977), p. 600.

CHAPTER 3: *The Affinities of Film: The Realm of the Everyday*

1. Roland Barthes, *Mythologies* (New York: Hill and Wang, 1972), p. 11.

CHAPTER 5: *The Affinities of Film: Mythologies of Consciousness*

1. In *Film: A Montage of Theories*, ed. Richard D. MacCann (New York: Dutton, 1966), pp. 203–204.
2. "Stylistic Devices" (1919); reprinted in *Russian Formalism*, ed. S. Bann and J. E. Bowlt (Edinburgh: Scottish Academic Press, 1973), p. 48.

CHAPTER 6: *The Language of Indirectness: Metaphoric Writing*

1. "The Poetics of Film" (1913); reprinted in *Filmkultura* (Budapest), 1975.
2. Interview in the *San Francisco Chronicle*.
3. Marshall McLuhan, *Understanding Media* (New York: McGraw-Hill, 1964), p. VII.

Bibliography

Adorno, Theodor W. *Philosophy of Modern Music*. New York: Seabury, 1973.

Aristotle. *Poetics*. New York: Hill & Wang, 1961.

Arnheim, Rudolf. *Art and Visual Perception: A Psychology of the Creative Eye*. Berkeley: University of California Press, 1954.

———. *Film as Art*. London: Faber & Faber, 1958.

———. *Toward a Psychology of Art*. Berkeley: University of California Press, 1966.

———. *Visual Thinking*. Berkeley: University of California Press, 1969.

Balázs, Béla. *Filmkultura*. Budapest: Gondolat, 1948.

Bann, S., and Bowlt, J. E., eds. *Russian Formalism*. Edinburgh: Scottish Academic Press, 1973.

Barthes, Roland. *Elements of Semiology*. Translated by Annette Laversy and Colin Smith. New York: Hill & Wang, 1967.

———. *L'Empire des signes*. Paris: Skira, 1970.

———. *Mythologies*. Translated by Annette Laversy. New York: Hill & Wang, 1972.

———. *The Pleasure of the Text*. Translated by Richard Miller. New York: Hill & Wang, 1975.

———. *Système de la mode*. Paris: Seuil, 1967.

———. *S-Z*. Translated by Richard Miller. New York: Hill & Wang, 1975.

———. *Writing Degree Zero*. New York: Hill & Wang, 1977.

Baudrillard, Jean. *L'Echange symbolique et la mort*. Paris: Gallimard, 1976.

———. *Le Système des objets*. Paris: Gallimard, 1968.

Bazin, André. *What Is Cinema?* Translated by Hugh Gray. Berkeley: University of California Press, 1967.

Benedict, Ruth. *Patterns of Culture*. New York: New American Library, 1934.

Benjamin, Walter. *Illuminations*. Edited by Hannah Arendt. New York: Harcourt, Brace, 1968.

———. *Reflections: Essays, Aphorisms, Autobiographical Writings*. Translated by Edmund Jephcott. New York: Harcourt Brace Jovanovich, 1973.

Bentley, Eric. *The Playwright as Thinker*. New York: Harcourt, Brace, 1967.

Benveniste, Emile. *Problemes de linguistique générale*. Paris: Gallimard. 1966.

Bergson, Henri. *Matter and Memory*. New York: Humanities Press, 1970.

Berne, Eric. *Games People Play*. New York: Grove Press, 1964.

Bettelheim, Bruno. *The Uses of Enchantment: The Meaning and Importance of Fairy Tales*. New York: Knopf, 1976.

Bettetini, Gianfranco. *Cinema: lingua e scrittura*. Milan: Bompiani, 1968.

———. *The Language and Technique of the Film*. The Hague: Mouton, 1973.

Bluestone, George. *Novels into Film: The Metamorphosis of Fiction into Cinema*. Berkeley: University of California Press, 1957.

Brecht, Bertolt. *Arbeitjournal*. Frankfurt: Suhrkamp, 1973.

Burch, Noel. *Praxis du cinema*. Paris: Gallimard, 1969.

Cage, John. *Silence*. Middleton, Ct.: Wesleyan University Press, 1961.

Caillois, Roger. *Mythologie*. Paris: Gallimard.

Cassirer, Ernst. *Language and Myth*. Translated by Susanne K. Langer. New York: Dover, 1946.

———. *The Philosophy of Symbolic Forms*. Vol. 3. *The Phenomenology of Knowledge*. Translated by Ralph Manheim. New Haven: Yale University Press, 1957.

Chatman, Seymour B. *Story and Discourse: Narrative Structure in Fiction and Film*. Ithaca: Cornell University Press, 1978.

Chomsky, Noam. *Cartesian Linguistics*. New York: Harper & Row, 1966.

———. *Language and Mind*. New York: Harcourt, Brace, 1968.

De Saussure, Ferdinand. *Course in General Linguistics*. Translated by Wade Baskin. New York: McGraw-Hill, 1966.

Eco, Umberto. *A Theory of Semiotics*. Bloomington: Indiana University Press, 1978.

Eisenstein, Sergei. *Film Form*. New York: Harcourt, Brace, 1969.

———. *Film Sense*. New York: Harcourt, Brace, 1969.

Eisner, Lotte. *The Haunted Screen: Expressionism in the German Cinema and the Influence of Max Reinhardt*. Translated by Roger Greaves. Berkeley: University of California Press, 1969.

Eliade, Mircea. *The Myth of the Eternal Return*. Translated by Willard R. Trask. Princeton: Princeton University Press, 1954.

Esslin, Martin. *The Theatre of the Absurd*. New York: Doubleday, 1969.

Etiemble, Etienne. *L'Ecriture*. Paris: Gallimard, 1973.

Foucault, Michel. *Les Mots et les choses*. Paris: Gallimard, 1966.

Francastel, Pierre. *Etudes de sociologie de l'art*. Paris: Denoel, 1970.

Freud, Sigmund. *Character and Culture*. New York: Macmillan, 1963.

———. *Civilization and Its Discontents*. Edited and translated by James Strachey. New York: W. W. Norton, 1962.

———. *Jokes and Their Relation to the Unconscious*. Translated by James Strachey. New York: W. W. Norton, 1963.

———. *The Psychopathology of Everyday Life*. Edited by James Strachey. Translated by Alan Tyson. New York: W. W. Norton, 1971.

———. *Totem and Taboo*. Standard edition. Translated by James Strachey. New York: W. W. Norton, 1952.

Fulchignoni, Enrico. *La civilisation des images*. Paris: Payot, 1969.

Gans, Herbert J. *Popular Culture and High Culture: An Analysis and Evaluation of Taste*. New York: Basic Books, 1975.

Genette, Gérard. *Figures*. Paris: Seuil, 1966.

Gibson, James. *The Perception of the Visual World*. Boston: Houghton Mifflin, 1950.

———. *The Senses Considered As Perceptual Systems*. Boston: Houghton Mifflin, 1966.
Goffman, Erving. *Interactional Ritual: Essays on Face-to-Face Behavior*. New York: Doubleday, 1967.
———. *The Presentation of Self in Everyday Life*. New York: Doubleday, 1959.
———. *Strategic Interaction*. Philadelphia: University of Pennsylvania Press, 1969.
Goldmann, Lucien. *La sociologie du roman*. Paris: Gallimard, 1964.
Gombrich, Ernst H. *Art and Illusion: A Study in the Psychology of Pictorial Presentation*. 2d ed. Princeton: Princeton University Press, 1961.
Gregory, R. L. *Eye and Brain*. New York: McGraw-Hill, 1966.
———. *The Intelligent Eye*. New York: McGraw-Hill, 1970.
Gregory, R. L., and Gombrich, E. H. *Illusion in Nature and Art*. New York: Charles Scribner's Sons, 1974.
Greimas, A. J. *Du Sens: essais sémiotiques*. Paris: Seuil, 1970.
———. *Semantique structurale*. Paris: Larousse, 1966.
Hall, Edward T. *Beyond Culture*. New York: Doubleday, 1977.
———. *The Hidden Dimension*. New York: Doubleday, 1966.
———. *The Silent Language*. New York: Doubleday, 1959.
Harcourt, Peter. *Six European Directors*. London: Penguin, 1974.
Henderson, Brian. *A Critique of Film Theory*. New York: Dutton, 1980.
Hjelmslev, Louis. *Essais linguistiques*. Paris: Minuit, 1971.
Hochberg, Julian, and Brooks, Virginia. "The Perception of Motion Pictures." In *Handbook of Perception*, vol. X. *Perceptual Ecology*. New York: Academic Press, 1978.
Jakobson, Roman. *Essais de linguistique générale*. Paris: Minuit, 1963.
———. *Questions de poétique*. Paris: Seuil, 1973.
James, William. *The Principles of Psychology*. New York: Dover, 1950.
Jung, Carl G. *Man and His Symbols*. London: Aldus Books, 1964.
Kepes, Gyorgy. *The Language of Vision*. Chicago: Paul Theobald, 1945.
———, ed. *Sign, Image and Symbol*. London: Studio Vista, 1966.
Kermode, Frank. *The Sense of an Ending: Studies in the Theory of Fiction*. New York: Oxford University Press, 1968.
Kitses, John. *Horizons West: Studies in Authorship in the Western Film*. Bloomington: Indiana University Press, 1970.
Koestler, A. *The Act of Creation*. London: Hutchinson, 1964.
Koffka, Kurt. *Principles of Gestalt Psychology*. New York: Harcourt, Brace, 1935.
Kracauer, Sigfried. *From Caligari to Hitler: A Psychological History of the German Film*. Princeton: Princeton University Press, 1967.
———. *The Nature of Film*. New York: Oxford University Press, 1960.
Kristeva, Julia. *Recherches sur une semanalyse*. Paris: Seuil, 1969.
Laffay, Albert. *Logique du cinéma: création et spectacle*. Paris: Masson, 1964.
Langer, Susanne K. *Philosophy in a New Key: A Study in the Symbolism of Reason, Rite and Art*. 3d ed. Cambridge: Harvard University Press, 1957.
Lessing, G. E. *Laocoon*. Boston: Little, Brown, 1910.
Lévi-Strauss, Claude. *The Raw and the Cooked: An Introduction to a Science of Mythology*. New York: Harper & Row, 1970.
———. *The Savage Mind*. Chicago: University of Chicago Press, 1966.

———. *Structural Anthropology*. New York: Basic Books, 1963.

Levy-Bruhl, Lucien. *L'Ame primitive*. Paris: Alcan, 1927.

———. *Les fonctions mentales dans les societes inferieures*. Paris: Alcan, 1918.

Lewin, Kurt. *Principles of Topological Psychology*. New York: McGraw-Hill, 1936.

Lherminier, Pierre, ed. *L'Art du cinéma*. Paris: Seghers, 1950.

Liehm, Mira, and Liehm, Antonin. *The Most Important Art: East European Film after 1945*. Berkeley: University of California Press, 1977.

Lindekens, R. *Essais de semiotique visuelle*. Paris: Klincksieck, 1976.

Lotman, Jurij. *Semiotics of Cinema*. Ann Arbor: Michigan Slavic Publications, 1976.

Lukács, Gorgy. *Esztetika*. Budapest: Akademiai Kiado, 1970.

McLuhan, Marshall. *The Gutenberg Galaxy: The Making of Typographic Man*. Toronto: University of Toronto Press, 1962.

———. *Understanding Media: The Extensions of Man*. New York: McGraw-Hill, 1964.

Marcorelles, Louis. *Le Cinéma direct*. Paris.

Marin, Louis. "La Description de l'image." *Communciations* (Paris) 15 (1970).

Mast, Gerald, and Cohen, Marshall. *Film Theory and Criticism*. New York: Oxford University Press, 1979.

Mauss, Marcel. *A General Theory of Magic*. Translated by Robert Brain. New York: Norton, 1972.

———. *Sociologie et anthropologie*. Paris: P.U.F., 1950.

Mérei, Ferenc. *Gyermeklelektani vizsgalatok*. Budapest: Gondolat.

Merleau-Ponty, Maurice. *Phenomenology of Perception*. Translated by Colin Smith. New York: Humanities Press, 1962.

———. *Signs*. Translated by Richard C. McCleary. Evanston: Northwestern University Press, 1964.

Metz, Christian. *Essais sur la signification au cinéma*. Paris: Klincksieck, 1968.

———. *Film Language: A Semiotics of the Cinema*. Translated by Michael Taylor. New York: Oxford University Press, 1974.

———. *The Imaginary Signifier*. Translated by C. Britton, A. Williams, B. Brewster, and A. Gruzzetti. Bloomington: Indiana University Press, 1982.

———. *Language and Cinema*. Translated by Donna Umiker-Sebeok. The Hague: Mouton, 1974.

Mitry, Jean. *Esthétique et psychologie du cinéma*. 2 vols. Paris: Éditions Universitaires, 1963–65.

Moholy-Nagy, László. *Painting, Photography, and Film*. Cambridge: MIT Press, 1969.

———. *Vision in Motion*. Chicago: Paul Theobald, 1947.

Moles, Abraham. *Information Theory and Esthetic Perception*. Translated by Joel E. Cohen. Urbana: University of Illinois Press, 1966.

Morin, Edgar. *Le Cinéma ou l'homme imaginaire*. Paris: Minuit, 1956.

———. *The Stars*. Translated by Richard Howard. New York: Grove Press, 1960.

Morris, Charles. *Writings on the General Theory of Signs*. The Hague: Mouton, 1971.

Mounin, G. *Introduction à la sémiologie*. Paris: Minuit, 1970.

Murray, Henry A., ed. *Myth and Mythmaking*. Boston: Beacon Press, 1968.
Nichols, Bill, ed. *Movies and Methods*. Berkeley: University of California Press, 1977.
Osgood, Charles E., and Sebeok, Thomas A. *Psycholinguistics*. Bloomington: Indiana University Press, 1963.
Panofsky, Erwin. *Meaning in the Visual Arts*. New York: Doubleday, 1955.
Pasolini, Pier P. *Empirismo Eretico*. Milan: Garzanti, 1972.
———. *Pasolini on Pasolini*. London: Thames and Hudson, 1969.
Peirce, Charles S. *Collected Papers*. Cambridge: Harvard University Press, 1958.
Piaget, Jean. *The Child's Conception of the World*. New York: Humanities Press, 1960.
———. *The Language and Thought of the Child*. New York: New American Library, 1955.
———. *Mechanisms of Perception*. Translated by G. N. Seagrin. New York: Basic Books, 1969.
———. *The Psychology of Intelligence*. London: Routledge & Kegan Paul, 1971.
———. *Structuralism*. New York: Basic Books, 1970.
Piaget, Jean, and Inhelder, Barbel. *The Psychology of the Child*. Translated by Helen Weaver. New York: Basic Books, 1969.
Propp, Vladimir. *Morphology of the Folktale*. The Hague: Mouton, 1958.
Pudovkin, Vsevolod, I. *Film Technique and Film Acting*. Edited and translated by Ivor Montagu. New York: Grove Press, 1970.
Robbe-Grillet, Alain. *For a New Novel: Essays on Fiction*. Translated by Richard Howard. New York: Grove Press, 1966.
Rohmer, Eric. *La conception de l'espace chez Murnau*. Paris: Union Générale d'Éditions.
Sapir, Edward. *Language: An Introduction to the Study of Speech*. New York: Harcourt, Brace, 1921.
Schaff, Adam. *Introduction to Semantics*. London: Pergamon Press, 1962.
Sebeok, Thomas A. *Animal Communication*. Bloomington: Indiana University Press, 1968.
Simmel, Georg. *The Conflict in Modern Culture and Other Essays*. New York: Teachers College Press, 1968.
Sitney, P. Adams, ed. *The Essential Cinema: Essays on Films in the Collection of the Anthology Film Archives*. New York: New York University Press, 1974.
Sontag, Susan. *Against Interpretation*. Farrar, Straus & Giroux, 1966.
———. *On Photography*. New York: Farrar, Straus & Giroux, 1977.
Szasz, Thomas S. *The Myth of Mental Illness: Foundations of a Theory of Personal Conduct*. Rev. ed. New York: Harper & Row, 1974.
Szondi, Peter. *Theorie Des Modernen Dramas*. Frankfurt: Suhrkamp, 1969.
Todorov, Tzvetan. *Littérature et signification*. Paris: Larousse, 1967.
———, ed. *Textes des formalistes russes*. Paris: Seuil, 1965.
Valéry, Paul. *Introduction a la poetique*. Paris: Gallimard, 1936.
Vygotsky, Lev S. *Thought and Language*. Edited by Gertrude Vakar. Translated by Eugenia Hanfmann. Cambridge: MIT Press, 1962.
Wellek, René, and Warren, Austin. *Theory of Literature*. Rev. ed. New York: Harcourt, Brace, 1956.
Werner, Heinz. *Comparative Psychology of Mental Development*. New York: International Universities Press, 1970.

Whorf, Benjamin. *Language, Thought and Reality*. Cambridge: MIT Press, 1948.
Wittgenstein, Ludwig. *Tractatus Logico-Philosophicus*. London: Kegan Paul, 1922.
Wollen, Peter. *Signs and Meaning in the Cinema*. Bloomington: Indiana University Press, 1972.
Wood, Michael. *America in the Movies*. New York: Delta Books, 1976.

Index